JOURNEY TO NEXT LEVEL ABUNDANCE

FINANCIAL LITERACY FOR ADULTS OF ALL AGES

GET READY, BE READY TO RECEIVE

LINDA BELL KENNEDY

AUTHOR OF BECOMING AN EMPOWERED ADULT

Contents

ABOUT THE AUTHOR

Linda Bell-Kennedy is an author, life strategist, and thought leader dedicated to helping individuals achieve financial freedom. With over three decades of experience in securities, business acquisitions, and commercial real estate investments, Linda encourages adults and families to take control of their money, seize opportunities to level up, and believe abundance is possible.

Born and raised in Los Angeles, Linda developed an early interest in personal finance after witnessing the impact of financial literacy among her more prominent family members (relatives who lived abundant lives on the other side of the tracks.)

Linda's approach to personal finance is straightforward and relatable, making financial concepts simple and accessible to everyone. As a firm believer in financial education, Linda is committed to teaching others how to make smart money decisions to improve the quality of their lives.

When not writing, Linda enjoys interior decorating, event planning, physical fitness, music, and business development. She actively practices mindfulness, and vibrational alignment to assist in manifesting aspirations.

Becoming an Empowered Adult is Linda's debut book, focusing on self-empowerment or personal empowerment, i.e., taking control of your own life. The current book *Journey to Next Level Abundance* shares real-life experiences to motivate, encourage, and inspire readers to realize possibilities and opportunities on their journey to financial independence.

To connect with Linda or learn more about her work, visit her website www.LindabTheBrand.com or follow her on Instagram www.instagram.com/lindab_the_brand/

INTRODUCTION

GET READY, **BE** READY ..... ***TO RECEIVE***.

This book is written for everyday people with the intention of adding **value** and improving the quality of life. It offers solutions to financial problems – solutions to get you from where you are to where you want to be financially – solutions to help you achieve financial goals such as:

- Producing multiple streams of income
- Owning rental property
- Operating a family-owned business
- Learning principles and techniques to generate income-producing assets
- Generating dividends, profit, and rental income to become a high-net-worth achiever

Solving problems related to personal finances requires the application of tools. These four tools, when implemented, are essential to achieving financial goals.

Here is a description of the four tools:

1. Creating a mindset that cultivates abundance, increase, growth, plenty, prosperity, cash flow, profit, gain, and assets.

2. Establishing income-producing habits, i.e., reading, learning, researching, following through, being consistent.

3. Expanding your vision to think big, dream big. FEEL as though what you desire [to have, to experience, to become] is ALREADY SO with the practice of envisioning and imagining. Note: Everything that has ever been created or produced was first imagined before it became a reality.

4. Recognizing and understanding the value of an opportunity.
   Seizing financial opportunities is crucial on the journey to next level abundance. Ultimately, the true value of an opportunity is realized with a willingness to learn and then take consistent action on what you've learned. Embracing opportunities can lead to significant achievements such as investing in real estate, stocks, or starting a business.

The following opportunities are stepping stones to achieve next-level abundance. Each opportunity is designed to assist you in achieving your goals, prompting you to start where you are, use what you have, and do what you can.

- ✓ Cultivating an Abundance Mindset
- ✓ Entry-Level Opportunity
- ✓ Opportunity to Level UP
- ✓ Head Start Opportunity
- ✓ Opportunity to Prosper
- ✓ Opportunity to Thrive

This book is written for adults, families, and the community – those who:

- Want to get their finances in order to purchase property.
- Possess a strong desire to experience abundance.
- Are determined to live a life of prosperity.
- Have decided they will no longer tolerate lack.
- Are living beyond their means, living from paycheck to paycheck.
- Are ready to learn and execute success strategies.
- Believe they can and will level up financially.

CHAPTER 1:
CULTIVATING AN ABUNDANCE MINDSET

An abundance mindset is the opposite of a scarcity mindset. Scarcity means, "To be without or to not have enough of something." Mindset is defined as "A way of thinking that influences a person's behavior, decisions, and responses to situations." Having a scarcity mindset is thinking about lack or not having enough of something to the point that it affects an individual's personal and professional life.

Since scarcity is caused by continuous thoughts of lack, it seems only reasonable if you want to experience abundance; you must change your mental focus by changing your thoughts and developing a new mindset - an abundance mindset that will attract abundant outcomes.

An abundance mindset is the belief that opportunities, resources, and success are plentiful rather than scarce. Cultivating an abundance mindset will require a different way of thinking. It's an opportunity to expand, to grow, to increase.

A person with an abundance mindset possesses several key qualities and attributes, including gratitude, optimism, generosity, confidence, open-mindedness, collaboration, continuous learning, and faith in abundance.

Call to Action:

Be Grateful. Appreciate all that you have. Focus on blessings rather than lack. Start and end the day with gratitude taking a moment each morning and night to reflect on things you are thankful for sets a positive tone. Keep a gratitude journal; writing down things you are thankful for each day fosters a habit of appreciation.

Be Optimistic. Being optimistic helps you believe that resources, success, and possibilities are plentiful rather than scarce. With this perspective, you're able to view challenges as opportunities, knowing that setbacks are temporary learning experiences. Being optimistic allows you to see opportunities rather than limitations and believe in the possibility and potential for growth.

Be Generous. Those with an abundance mindset give freely—whether through time, money, or knowledge—trusting that what they share will return in some form. Being generous is closely tied to an abundance mindset because it reflects the belief that there is more than enough to go around. When people give freely, they demonstrate confidence that their own needs will continue to be met. This creates a positive cycle of giving and receiving.

Be Confident. Being confident means trusting in yourself and your abilities, even in the face of uncertainty. It's about believing that you are capable of overcoming challenges and achieving your goals. Self-assurance allows you to make decisions without excessive doubt, stand firm in your values, and pursue opportunities with conviction. When you have confidence, you project strength and positivity, inspiring both yourself and those around you to embrace growth and success.

Be Open-minded. When you are open-minded, you are more willing to explore different paths to success rather than believing resources or opportunities are scarce. An open mind allows you to see possibilities, embrace new perspectives, and adapt to opportunities. By staying open to new possibilities, you recognize that growth and learning are continuous, reinforcing the belief that there is always more to achieve and discover.

Be Willing to Collaborate. To collaborate means to work together with others to achieve a common goal or create something meaningful. It involves sharing ideas, skills, and efforts in a cooperative and productive way. Effective collaboration requires communication, mutual respect, and a willingness to consider different perspectives to reach the best possible outcome.

Be a Continuous Learner. An abundance mindset and being a continuous learner are closely connected because both focus on growth, possibilities, and the belief that knowledge and opportunities are limitless. Being a continuous learner allows you to expand your knowledge and skills over time. It fosters personal and professional growth by keeping your mind open to new ideas, perspectives, and opportunities.

Have Faith in Abundance. A believe there is more than enough success, wealth, and happiness to go around reflects the mindset that resources and opportunities are not finite. It encourages the idea that everyone has the potential to achieve their goals and experience abundance in various forms. When we embrace this belief, we open ourselves to greater possibilities, knowing that the success of others does not take away from our own, and there's plenty to go around for everyone willing to pursue it.

SUMMARY: Developing these attributes, qualities, and characteristics will be beneficial in creating an abundance mindset.

The Law of Attraction states that like attracts like, meaning our thoughts and words influence the reality we experience. The objective here is to cultivate an abundance mindset to experience the quality of life you desire. To achieve what you desire, your thoughts and feelings must be a vibrational match with the abundance you desire.

Everything in the material world that a person wants or desires is fundamentally energy vibrating at different frequencies. Human beings also emit vibrational frequencies through their thoughts and emotions. Each and every thought carries an energetic vibration. Positive thoughts, such as love, gratitude, abundance, and confidence, generate high-frequency vibrations, while fear, doubt, lack, and negativity emit lower vibrations. What you focus your thoughts on mentally tends to manifest in your life.

Empowering Thoughts Attract Abundance

To achieve the abundance that you desire, your thoughts and feelings must be a vibrational match with whatever it is you desire. A person can emit vibrational frequencies to attract abundance by consciously aligning their thoughts and actions with prosperity. By consistently radiating high-frequency thoughts and feelings, you create the perfect environment for abundance to flow into your life.

Journaling is a written expression of thoughts, a recording of personal reflections and ideas. Journaling is a powerful tool for manifestation because it helps you focus your thoughts and intentions with clarity. By writing down your desires, you reinforce them in your subconscious mind, making it easier to align your actions and energy with your goals. It also allows you to track progress, recognize limiting beliefs, and replace them with empowering thoughts.

Example of Empowering Thoughts Recorded in a Daily Journal

Day 1: "***Opportunities for abundance are always around me.*** *Today, I noticed how many ways abundance flows into my life. Whether it's through unexpected blessings, new ideas, or connections with inspiring people, opportunities are everywhere. I feel excited knowing that every day presents new chances to grow, succeed, and receive the wealth that is meant for me."*

Day 2: ***"I see money as a tool that supports my best life.*** *Instead of worrying about finances, I choose to view money as an ally. It allows me to create experiences, take care of my loved ones, and invest in my dreams. Every dollar that comes to me carries potential, and I trust that my financial situation is always improving."*

Day 3: "***Abundance is a natural part of my life.*** *Just like the air I breathe and the sunshine I enjoy, abundance is always available to me. I don't have to chase it or struggle to earn it. The universe is abundant, and I am an extension of that limitless energy. I allow myself to receive freely and without hesitation."*

Day 4: ***"I am surrounded by wealth in many forms.*** *Today, I realize how much wealth I already have beyond money—love from family and friends, knowledge that enriches me, and experiences that bring me joy. Recognizing these forms of abundance makes me feel rich and fulfilled, which naturally attracts more prosperity into my life."*

Day 5: ***"I am always in the right place at the right time.*** *Everything in my life is unfolding perfectly, even when I don't see the full picture yet. I trust that the right opportunities, people, and resources will show up when I need them. This belief gives me confidence and peace, allowing me to welcome abundance with open arms."*

Day 6: "Giving and receiving go hand in hand. I love the feeling of generosity—whether it's sharing my knowledge, time, or resources. I know that the more I give from a place of joy, the more I open myself up to receiving in return. Abundance flows effortlessly when I approach life with a giving heart."

Day 7: ***"I am always growing and evolving toward greater success.*** *Every challenge I face teaches me something valuable, making me wiser and stronger. Each step I take brings me closer to the life I envision. I trust in my ability to create wealth, happiness, and success because I am constantly learning and improving."*

Day 8: ***"I welcome abundance with ease and gratitude.*** *I don't have to overthink or force anything—abundance naturally flows into my life in expected and unexpected ways. I am open to receiving, and I trust that good things are always on their way to me. Life is abundant, and I am a magnet for prosperity."*

<ins>Summary</ins>: Through consistent journaling of your thoughts, you create a mindset of abundance, gratitude, and positivity, which naturally attracts more of what you desire into your life.

<ins>Call to Action</ins>: Make it a regular practice to think thoughts of abundance that shift your mindset to one of possibility, prosperity, and gratitude. When you focus on opportunities rather than limitations, you naturally attract more wealth, success, and joy into your life. Your thoughts create your reality, so by consistently thinking in ways that align with abundance—such as believing in endless opportunities, feeling grateful for what you have, and expecting financial growth—you open yourself up to receiving more. The more you train your mind to see abundance everywhere, the more effortlessly it flows into your life.

Feelings and Emotions Amplify Thoughts

The stronger the emotion attached to a thought (whether joy, fear, or gratitude), the more powerfully it is projected into the universe, influencing outcomes.

Taking deliberate action to feel the emotions associated with manifesting abundance helps align your energy with the prosperity you desire. When you cultivate feelings of gratitude, joy, confidence, and excitement, you raise your vibration, making it easier to attract wealth, opportunities, and success.

Act as if, feel as though what you desire is ALREADY SO. Practice imagining yourself already having what you desire. Pay close attention to how you feel, as this reveals the vibrational frequency of your thoughts.

Feeling abundant before it physically manifests signals to the universe that you are ready to receive, reinforcing a mindset of possibility rather than lack. By intentionally experiencing these emotions, you train your subconscious mind to expect abundance, making it a natural and effortless part of your life.

Call to Action

Feel A strong conviction that abundance is possible and already on its way.

Feel A deep appreciation for what you already have to attract more blessings.

Feel A sense of anticipation and joy about future opportunities and success.

Feel A high-vibrational state that aligns with attracting positive experiences.

Feel A calm assurance that abundance is unfolding in divine timing.

Feel In control of your destiny and the universe's ability to provide.

The Power of Spoken Words

Cultivating an abundance mindset includes the simple yet profound practice of speaking abundance into existence. By consciously choosing words that affirm abundance and gratitude, we gradually reprogram our mindset to attract and embrace greater prosperity. By consistently using empowering words, we rewire our brains to see opportunities even in adversity, reinforcing the belief that abundance is always within reach.

An abundance mindset is rooted in the belief that opportunities, resources, and success are plentiful rather than scarce. On the other hand, words of limitation, fear, and doubt can condition us to see the world through a lens of scarcity, where competition and lack dominate our thinking.

One of the most effective ways spoken words influence an abundance mindset is through affirmations and self-talk. When we verbalize statements such as "I am open to new opportunities," or "There is always more than enough to go around," we train our minds to focus on possibilities rather than limitations. This positive reinforcement not only boosts confidence but also shifts our energy, making us more receptive to success and prosperity.

Conversely, complaining, criticizing, or speaking negatively about money, success, or others' achievements can create a self-fulfilling cycle of scarcity and dissatisfaction that reinforces scarcity thinking, limiting our ability to recognize and seize opportunities.

Spoken words hold incredible power in shaping the reality we experience. By consciously choosing words that reflect abundance, we can reprogram our subconscious mind to expect growth, wealth, and fulfillment.

Affirmations for developing an abundance mindset

An affirmation is a positive, declarative statement that reinforces a desired belief, mindset, or outcome. It is used to reprogram the subconscious mind, boost confidence, and cultivate a positive outlook. Affirmations are often repeated daily to shift thought patterns, replace limiting beliefs, and align one's mindset with goals such as success, abundance, or self-improvement.

Call to Action:

Repeat affirmations and declarations to shape beliefs and subconscious programming, making certain outcomes more likely.

Here is a list of high-frequency words and affirmations that attract prosperity:

1. I am worthy of financial abundance.
2. Money flows to me effortlessly and abundantly.
3. I am open to unlimited wealth and success.
4. Opportunities for prosperity surround me every day.
5. I attract wealth with ease and joy.
6. Abundance is my natural state.
7. I am grateful for the prosperity in my life.
8. Financial success is inevitable for me.
9. I confidently make wise and profitable financial decisions.
10. My energy attracts wealth and abundance.

The spoken word is the verbal expression of thoughts, feelings, or beliefs. We use words to express what we think, feel, or believe. Words give form to thoughts, and thoughts shape our experiences and outcomes.

Call to Action

- Begin by shifting from a scarcity mentality to one of abundance, believing that wealth and opportunities are limitless and available to you.
- Practice positive affirmations such as, "Money flows to me easily and effortlessly," to reprogram your subconscious mind. Speak affirmations with conviction, such as, "I am a magnet for abundance" or "Prosperity flows effortlessly into my life."
- Visualize yourself already experiencing financial success, feeling the emotions of security, freedom, and joy as if they are your present reality. Avoid negative self-talk or doubts about money, as these lower your vibrational frequency and attract financial struggle. Practice visualization, vividly imagining yourself living in financial success while feeling the emotions of wealth and security.
- Surround yourself with uplifting influences—books, mentors, and environments that reinforce wealth consciousness.
- Lastly, take inspired action by seeking opportunities, making wise financial decisions, being open to learning, and continually seeking valuable knowledge.

CONCLUSION: CHAPTER 1 (CULTIVATING AN ABUNDANCE MINDSET)

What you think, feel, and speak consistently shapes your reality, as these elements align with the energy you emit, attracting similar frequencies back to you.

When your thoughts, emotions, words, and actions are in harmony with prosperity, you naturally attract financial abundance into your life.

CHAPTER 2:
ENTRY-LEVEL OPPORTUNITY

This level describes people who are currently living beyond their means, spending more than they earn, or living from paycheck to paycheck with little to no funds left over for unexpected emergencies or money to save and invest. Within this chapter are practical, realistic solutions and action steps to conquer and overcome poor spending habits, as illustrated by Sandra.

Hi, I'm Sandra. I work in the entertainment industry as a producer. I'm single with no children. I have a very active social life with my friends and co-workers. We frequently dine out at restaurants and meet up at bars for cocktails three to four times a week. Every other month I may take a weekend trip out of town.

Recently, I applied for a loan and was denied. It appears I'm often over-extended on my credit card limits.

I would like to be in a position to buy a house in the next year or two, but I'm unable to save for the downpayment.

What can I do to improve my finances?

Despite the fact that Sandra earns a decent salary, she still manages to live beyond her means, regularly overspends, and just gets by living from paycheck to paycheck.

<u>Living beyond one's means</u> is a common occurrence that affects many income groups, from low-income earners to high-net-worth individuals. Despite differences in income levels, the tendency to overspend relative to earnings or net income can stem from social pressures, the desire for instant gratification, or a lack of financial literacy.

For lower-income individuals, this often means using credit to cover basic necessities or occasional luxuries, leading to a cycle of borrowing and repayment that is difficult to escape. Middle-income earners might stretch their finances to afford homes, cars, and vacations that signal success, often relying on credit to maintain a certain way of life. Even high-income earners can fall into the trap of excessive spending, funding extravagant lifestyles that surpass their substantial incomes.

Overall, living beyond one's means can lead to financial instability, increased debt, and a lack of savings, ultimately undermining long-term financial security.

Excessive spending, characterized by consistently spending more than one earns or can afford, often leads to significant financial and personal challenges. This behavior can result in overwhelming debt, high interest payments, and a strained financial situation. The continuous cycle of overspending can prevent individuals from saving for future needs, investing, or building an emergency fund, leaving them financially vulnerable. Furthermore, the stress associated with excessive debt can impact mental health, relationships, and overall quality of life. Breaking the habit of excessive spending requires disciplined budgeting, a shift in mindset towards financial responsibility, and often, seeking professional financial advice.

Impulse Buying, is defined as a sudden feeling that drives a person to make an unplanned purchase for instant gratification or relief. Impulse buying is often prompted by an emotional trigger such as excitement, stress, or fear of missing out (FOMO).

Triggers for impulsive purchases can vary widely, but common ones include:

1. Emotional States: Feelings of stress, sadness, or boredom can lead to retail therapy as a way to seek comfort or distraction.
2. Sales and Discounts: The perception of getting a good deal can create a sense of urgency and justify spontaneous buying.
3. Advertising and Marketing: Targeted ads and persuasive marketing techniques can create a desire for products you hadn't previously considered.
4. Social Influences: Seeing friends or influencers buy certain items can trigger the urge to purchase the same things to fit in or keep up.
5. Convenience and Accessibility: Easy access to online shopping platforms and one-click purchasing options can make impulsive buying more tempting.
6. In-Store Triggers: Attractive store displays, product placements, and limited-time offers can encourage unplanned purchases.
7. Rewards Programs: Loyalty points, cashback offers, and other rewards can entice consumers to make impulsive purchases to earn more rewards.

Recognizing these triggers can help in developing strategies to avoid impulsive spending and stick to a budget.

Living from paycheck to paycheck, also known as spending all your earnings, is a financial reality for many individuals and families, where each month's income is immediately allocated to cover essential expenses, such as rent, utilities, groceries, and excessive debt payments. Without a financial cushion, even minor emergencies, like car repairs or medical bills, can lead to significant hardship. This lifestyle makes it difficult to plan for the future, achieve financial independence, or invest in opportunities.

SOLUTIONS OFFERED

As stated in the introduction, this book is written to offer solutions to financial problems – solutions to get you from where you are to where you want to be financially – solutions to help you improve the quality of your life.

Problems: living beyond your means, spending more than you earn, or living from paycheck to paycheck.

Solution: Get your finances in order by reducing debt, controlling your spending, and increasing your savings.

Step 1. Create a Spending Plan to determine how the money is being spent.

Step 2. Live on less than you make. Control your spending. Practice delayed gratification. Reduce your debts.

Step 3. Start or increase your savings.

Step 4 Create a Budgeting Strategy: The 70-10-10-10 approach to personal finances.

The Entry-Level Opportunity is the opportunity level in which you are ready to improve how you handle your personal finances **by starting where you are, using what you have, and doing what you can.**

Starting where you are: where are you currently?

At this level, you're in the place wherein you need to make smart decisions with money and get your personal finances in order to experience next-level abundance; you're ready to learn and execute success strategies to level up financially.

Using what you have: what do you actually have?

You have countless opportunities available, including a substantial supply of information, a wide range of educational resources, and training on the subject of personal finances.

Doing what you can: what can you do to make smart decisions relating to personal finances?

Get your finances in order by reducing debt, controlling your spending, and increasing your savings.

<u>DO WHAT YOU CAN</u>

Step 1. Create a Spending Plan (the first draft)

Creating a spending plan is a smart decision. It is a foundational tool for maintaining financial control and achieving long-term financial goals. It serves as a roadmap for managing income, expenses, and savings, ensuring that financial resources are allocated effectively.

By outlining specific spending categories and setting limits on "wants" and "needs," a spending plan helps you avoid overspending and identify areas where you can cut back. It also provides a clear picture of financial health, allowing for better decision-making and goal-setting.

Regularly reviewing and adjusting the spending plan can lead to improved financial discipline, reduced stress, and assist in planning and saving for future needs and emergencies. When your income and expenses are clearly laid out in a spending plan, you can easily see where the money is being spent.

Sample of a Personal Spending Plan

Category	Items Included	Description
Income		
$	Salary/Wages	Primary source of earnings from employment (net income).
$	Rental Income	Income generated from renting out property.
$	Investments	Dividends, interest, or capital gains from investments.
$	Side Hustle	Additional income from freelance work or part-time jobs.
Fixed Expenses		
$	Mortgage/Rent	Monthly payment for housing.
$	Property Taxes	Annual or semi-annual taxes on owned property.
$	Insurance (Health, Auto, Homeowners, etc.)	Monthly premiums for various types of insurance coverage.
$	Utilities (Electricity, Water, Gas, Internet, etc.)	Monthly bills for essential services.
$	Loan Payments (Car Loan, Student Loan, etc.)	Monthly payments towards loans.
$	Subscriptions (Netflix, Gym Membership, etc.)	Regular payments for subscriptions and memberships.
Flexible Expenses		
$	Groceries	Weekly or monthly spending on food and household items.
$	Transportation (Fuel, Public Transport, Car Maintenance)	Costs associated with commuting and vehicle upkeep.
$	Healthcare (Medications, Doctor Visits, etc.)	Out-of-pocket medical expenses not covered by insurance.

Category	Items Included	Description
$	Clothing and Personal Care	Purchases related to clothing, toiletries, and personal grooming.
$	Education (Books, Supplies, Courses, etc.)	Costs for educational materials and courses.
Discretionary Expenses		
$	Dining Out	Spending on meals at restaurants or takeout.
$	Entertainment (Movies, Concerts, Events, etc.)	Leisure activities such as movies, concerts, and other events.
$	Travel	Expenses related to vacations, trips, and getaways.
$	Hobbies	Costs associated with hobbies and recreational activities.
$	Gifts and Donations	Spending on gifts for others and charitable donations.
$	Miscellaneous	Miscellaneous spending not categorized elsewhere, including impulse buys and small indulgences.

This table provides a structured breakdown of expenses commonly found in a personal spending plan. It helps individuals or households manage their finances by categorizing income and expenses into fixed, flexible, and discretionary categories, thereby enabling better financial planning and decision-making. Adjustments can be made within each category based on individual circumstances and financial goals.

Instructions to Prepare a Personal Spending Plan

- Calculate your total net income.

  Some common sources of income include a weekly, bi-weekly, or monthly paycheck, Social Security payments, royalties, and investment income. Net income is the money that you actually have available to spend after-tax payments and pre-tax contributions have been deducted.

- Create a list of your total monthly expenses.

  Typically, there are three types of monthly expenses: fixed expenses, flexible expenses, and discretionary expenses.

  a. Fixed or reoccurring expenses: These are the necessary expenses that remain the same each month, including your rent, car payment, and insurance.

  b. Flexible expenses: These are the essential expenses that can vary each month, such as your utilities, clothes, and grocery bills.

  c. Discretionary or non-essential expenses: These are personal expenses where you have more control over what and how much to spend. A discretionary expense is a cost that a person can get by without, if necessary. This category can include things like trips to the coffee shop, going to the movies, and dining out at restaurants with friends. These expenses are often defined as things that are "wants," rather than "needs."

     Reducing your discretionary expenses and limiting your spending will free up the money needed to save on a consistent basis. Taking time to really think through the non-essential expenses and how to decrease them is the first step toward determining a monthly savings amount to be included in the spending plan.

Subtract your expenses from your income to determine the amount of money you have leftover to spend. If the amount leftover is close to zero or a negative number, review the spending plan to adjust your non-essential expenses. The items listed as discretionary expenses are easier to trim if you're spending too much or if that money is needed elsewhere.

With the first draft of the spending plan prepared listing all of the income and expenses, you're now able to track your actual spending habits and see where the money is going.

DO WHAT YOU CAN

Step 2. Live on less than you make. Practice delayed gratification. Control your spending. Eliminate discretionary expenses. Reduce your debts.

The five largest discretionary or non-essential expenses in the average family's budget typically include:

1. Dining Out and Entertainment: This category often includes expenses related to eating out at restaurants, ordering takeout, and going to movies, concerts, or other forms of entertainment.
2. Vacations and Travel: Costs associated with transportation, accommodations, meals, and activities during vacations or weekend getaways.
3. Subscription Services: Monthly or annual fees for streaming services, gym memberships, subscription boxes, and other discretionary subscriptions.

4. Hobbies and Recreational Activities: Expenses related to hobbies, such as sports equipment, craft supplies, musical instruments, or other leisure pursuits that require ongoing spending.
5. Clothing and Accessories: Purchases beyond basic clothing needs, including fashion items, shoes, accessories, and occasional wardrobe updates.

These expenses can vary widely depending on a person's lifestyle choices, geographic location, and family size, but they often represent significant discretionary spending in a household budget. Adjusting spending in these areas can help free up funds for reducing debts, savings, or other financial goals.

Reallocating discretionary or non-essential expenses to reduce debts can be a strategic move toward achieving financial freedom and reducing stress. Non-essential expenses, such as entertainment, dining out, hobbies, and leisure, often consume a significant portion of the budget without contributing to long-term financial goals. By redirecting these funds towards debt repayment, a person can accelerate the process of becoming debt-free. This approach not only decreases the principal amount owed but also reduces the interest paid over time, resulting in substantial savings. Prioritizing debt repayment can improve credit scores, increase financial stability, and provide a sense of accomplishment and control over one's finances.

<u>USE WHAT YOU HAVE</u>

The funds previously spent on discretionary or non-essential expenses and unnecessary items can now be used to reduce debt and pay off bills.

"WHAT IF" Scenarios to repurpose discretionary and non-essential expenses		
What if, you quit smoking cigarettes; [one pack a day at $8.00 a pack. By the end of the week, you would have $56; in two weeks $112; in one month $240; in one year $2920]		
Possible Amount to be Repurposed to Reduce or Pay Off Debts:		
Within 12 mos	Within 18 mos	Within 24 mos
$2920	$4320	$5840

Imagine this, the day has arrived, you've made your final car payment of $700 per month. Now is the time to make a smart money decision to redirect the $700 to reduce another debt or increase your savings.		
Possible Amount to be Repurposed to Reduce or Pay Off Debts:		
Within 12 mos	Within 18 mos	Within 24 mos
$8400	$12,600	$16,800

Your toddler is now potty-trained. Yay!!!!, The average cost for disposable diapers costing $75 per month is an expense you can transfer and redirect to another expense to reduce debts.		
Possible Amount to be Repurposed to Reduce or Pay Off Debts:		
Within 12 mos	Within 18 mos	Within 24 mos
$900	$1350	$1800

What if you limit your daily trips to your favorite coffee shop to every other day or four days a week. If your family's daily coffee shop order usually cost $19.00 that's a savings of $57 per week; $228 per month and $2736 a year when you limit your trips to the coffee shop to four times a week.		
Possible Amount to be Repurposed to Reduce or Pay Off Debts:		
Within 12 mos	Within 18 mos	Within 24 mos
$2736	$4104	$5472
Congratulations!!! Your child is graduating from daycare moving on to first grade in the public school district. For many parents, childcare costs approximately $800 a month. Once the child enters public school, this expense can be redirected to pay off or reduce another debt.		

Possible Amount to be Repurposed to Reduce or Pay Off Debts:		
Within 12 mos	Within 18 mos	Within 24 mos
$9600	$14,400	$19,200

Living on less than you make and reducing expenses often requires significant sacrifices that can challenge one's habits and lifestyle. It might mean cutting back on dining out, foregoing luxury items, or choosing more affordable alternatives for everyday purchases. These sacrifices demand a shift in mindset, prioritizing long-term financial stability over immediate gratification. It may also involve giving up certain conveniences, such as opting for public transportation instead of driving or canceling subscriptions and memberships that are not essential. While these changes can be difficult, especially at the beginning, they cultivate financial discipline and resilience. Ultimately, the sacrifices made to reduce expenses pave the way for greater financial freedom and the achievement of more substantial, long-term financial goals.

DO WHAT YOU CAN

Reduce Debt. Reducing debt is a key strategy for improving your credit score. Start by focusing on paying down high-interest credit card balances to lower your credit utilization ratio, which significantly impacts your score. Your credit utilization ratio is the amount of credit you're using compared to your total available credit.

It is calculated by dividing your total credit card balances by your total credit limits and multiplying by 100 to get a percentage. For example, if you have a total credit limit of $10,000 and your current balances amount to $2,500, your credit utilization ratio is 25%.

A lower credit utilization ratio is generally better for your credit score because it shows that you're not overly reliant on credit and can manage your credit responsibly. High utilization ratios can signal to lenders that you may be overextended and could be at higher risk of defaulting on your payments. Therefore, spreading out balances and keeping individual card utilization low can help maintain or improve your credit score.

By managing and gradually reducing your overall debt, you demonstrate responsible financial behavior, which is positively reflected in your credit score.

The best debts to pay off in full to improve your financial health and potentially boost your credit score are:

1. High-Interest Credit Card Debt: Paying off high-interest credit card debt is one of the most effective ways to improve your credit score and save money on interest payments. This also helps lower your credit utilization ratio, which can significantly boost your credit score.
2. Personal Loans: Personal loans often come with higher interest rates compared to secured loans. Paying them off can reduce your monthly financial obligations and free up funds for other expenses or savings.
3. Payday Loans: These loans typically carry extremely high interest rates and fees. Paying them off quickly can save you a substantial amount of money and prevent a cycle of debt.
4. Medical Debt: Although medical debt may be treated differently by credit scoring models, paying it off can prevent it from being sent to collections, which can severely impact your credit score.
5. Small Balances on Multiple Credit Cards: Paying off small balances on multiple credit cards can simplify your finances and reduce the number of accounts with outstanding balances, positively affecting your credit score.

6. Store Credit Cards: These often have higher interest rates compared to regular credit cards. Paying them off can help you avoid high-interest charges and improve your credit utilization ratio.
7. Home Equity Lines of Credit (HELOCs): If you have variable interest rates on a HELOC, paying it off can protect you from rising interest rates and reduce your overall debt load.
8. Auto Loans: If you have a high-interest auto loan, paying it off early can save you money on interest and improve your debt-to-income ratio, which can be beneficial if you're planning to apply for a mortgage or other significant credit in the future.

While paying off any debt is beneficial, prioritizing high-interest and unsecured debts can provide the most immediate financial relief and positive impact on your credit score.

DO WHAT YOU CAN

Consistently making on-time payments reduces the risk of late fees and negative marks on your credit report. Additionally, paying off smaller balances on multiple accounts can streamline your finances and reduce the number of accounts with outstanding debt. Aim to use less than 30% of your available credit. Regularly check your credit report for errors and dispute any inaccuracies with the credit bureaus. Avoid opening too many new accounts in a short period, as each credit application can result in a hard inquiry, which may lower your score temporarily.

Maintain a mix of credit types, such as credit cards, installment loans, and retail accounts, to demonstrate your ability to manage various forms of credit responsibly. Lastly, keep older accounts open to lengthen your credit history, which positively impacts your score over time.

$ $

How credit affects everyday life

Credit affects many aspects of one's life, often in ways that extend beyond just financial transactions. A good credit score opens doors to favorable loan terms, lower interest rates, and higher credit limits, which can make significant purchases like homes and cars more affordable. It can also influence rental applications, as landlords often use credit scores to gauge a tenant's reliability. Even job prospects can be affected, as employers in certain industries review credit reports during the hiring process. Additionally, a good credit score can lead to lower insurance premiums and better terms for utility services, saving money in the long run. Conversely, a poor credit score can result in higher costs, denied applications, and limited financial opportunities, making it harder to achieve financial goals. In essence, credit serves as a key indicator of financial trustworthiness, impacting various aspects of everyday life.

USE WHAT YOU HAVE. You now have valuable information and knowledge to be applied to your spending plan that will assist in reducing debts. When knowledge is applied, it fosters continuous improvement in your personal finances, enabling you to solve problems and make informed decisions. Applied knowledge can lead to improved outcomes and the development of new skills. It involves taking principles and concepts learned through education or experience and implementing them in practical situations to achieve tangible results.

DO WHAT YOU CAN. Review and revise the spending plan often to reflect your intention to transfer funds from discretionary expenses to reduce or pay off specific debt amounts. In other words, the money that you used to spend on non-essential expenses or unnecessary items is now used to reduce or pay off debts.

Let's say, for example, you decide to limit your trips to the coffee shop to every other day, and you want to transfer and apply the funds to the payment of your retail jewelry store account for which you owe $2500. By paying the jewelry store an extra $57 per week, $228 per month, the jewelry store account will be paid in full in less than twelve months.

A spending plan is a "reference document" that will change with your needs and situation. Your spending plan should be flexible enough to change with whatever life changes come your way.

<u>Tools required to prepare an effective spending plan</u>

- A new and improved mindset
- Discipline
- Self-awareness
- Self-control
- Prioritizing
- Patience
- Consistency

To control spending, a disciplined mindset is crucial. This involves cultivating self-awareness to recognize triggers for impulsive purchases and developing self-control to resist unnecessary spending. Prioritizing long-term financial goals over immediate gratification is key, as is maintaining a realistic budget and regularly tracking expenses. Embracing a minimalist approach and finding contentment in what one already has can also help curb the urge to overspend. Lastly, being patient and understanding that financial stability requires consistent effort and smart decision-making is essential.

<u>USE WHAT YOU HAVE</u>

Step 3. Start growing your savings using funds from eliminated debts.

The chart below illustrates that it is possible to have a dedicated savings routine that fosters a mindset of prioritizing long-term financial goals over short-term gratification. Regularly increasing savings cultivates disciplined financial habits and instills a sense of control and confidence over one's financial future.

Former car payment		**Savings Account**		
		Month	Deposit Amount	Savings Account Balance
$700		1	$700	$700
$700		2	$700	$1400
$700		3	$700	$2100
$700		4	$700	$2800
$700		5	$700	$3500
$700		6	$700	$4200
$700		7	$700	$4900
$700		8	$700	$5600
$700		9	$700	$6300
$700		10	$700	$7000
$700		11	$700	$7700
$700		12	$700	$8400
$700		18	$700	$12,600
$700		**24**	$700	**$16,800**

Increasing one's savings account is vital for financial stability and future planning. A robust savings account acts as a safety net, providing security against unexpected expenses such as medical emergencies, car repairs, or job loss, thereby reducing the reliance on high-interest debt.

A healthy savings balance enables individuals to seize opportunities, whether it's starting a business, investing in real estate, or purchasing a home.

Saving with the intention to invest brings a multitude of advantages that can significantly enhance one's financial well-being. Investing is a powerful strategy to make your money work for you, transforming your earned income into a source of additional earnings. Instead of merely saving money, investing allows your capital to grow and generate returns through interest, dividends, and capital gains. By systematically setting aside funds designated for investments, this strategic approach allows for the growth of wealth through various investment vehicles such as stocks, bonds, mutual funds, or real estate, leveraging the power of compounding interest over time.

USE WHAT YOU HAVE

As a result of completing Steps 1, 2, and 3:

- You have learned to make smart money decisions by reducing debt, controlling your spending, and increasing your savings while understanding the benefits and advantages of investing.
- We are introducing you to the 70-10-10-10 approach to personal finances to be used in conjunction with the Personal Spending Plan in an effort to assist you in getting your finances in order.

DO WHAT YOU CAN

Step 4. Create a budgeting strategy based on the 70-10-10-10 approach to personal finances.

The 70-10-10-10 approach to personal finances is a budgeting strategy that divides an individual's income into four distinct categories to ensure a balanced and disciplined financial plan. Here's a breakdown of this method:

1. 70% for Living Expenses: The largest portion, 70% of the income, is allocated for essential living expenses. This includes housing, utilities, groceries, transportation, insurance, and other day-to-day necessities. The goal is to cover all the essential costs of living within this percentage, encouraging mindful spending and prioritization of needs over wants.

2. 10% for Savings: The next 10% is dedicated to savings. This can be for building an emergency fund, saving for short-term goals, or creating a financial cushion. Having a dedicated portion for savings ensures that individuals are consistently setting aside money for unforeseen circumstances or future needs.

3. 10% for Investing: Another 10% is allocated for investments. This could be in the stock market, real estate, retirement accounts, or other investment vehicles. Investing a portion of the income helps in growing wealth over time and achieving long-term financial goals through the power of compounding returns.

4. 10% for Giving or Charity: The final 10% is earmarked for giving or charitable contributions. This can include donations to charities, support for community projects, or helping out family and friends in need. Allocating a portion for giving fosters a sense of generosity and social responsibility, contributing to the well-being of others and supporting causes that one is passionate about.

By following the 70-10-10-10 approach, individuals can maintain a balanced financial life, ensuring that their immediate needs are met while also preparing for the future.

CONCLUSION: CHAPTER 2 (ENTRY-LEVEL OPPORTUNITY)

Smart money decisions refer to financial choices that are well-informed, strategic, and aligned with one's long-term financial goals. These decisions involve careful planning, budgeting, and prioritization to ensure that spending, saving, and investing activities contribute to overall financial health. By making smart money decisions, individuals can achieve financial stability, grow their wealth, and secure a comfortable future. These decisions are characterized by a proactive approach to managing finances, emphasizing the importance of consistency and discipline.

Smart money decisions include living within one's means, avoiding unnecessary debt, controlling your spending, increasing savings, building an emergency fund, investing wisely, and continuously educating oneself about personal finance.

CHAPTER 3:
OPPORTUNITY TO LEVEL UP

This opportunity level is for people who desire to acquire rental income property.

Throughout this book, we will introduce you to several working adults who share their journey to the next level of abundance, illustrating what is truly possible when your intentions and actions are in alignment.

We will continue with Nicole, a single mom, who describes her journey to Level UP from renter to real estate investor and landlord.

"Hi, I'm Nicole. I'd like to start by sharing information about my background.

It's always been my dream to own property. Growing up as a child, we lived in a low-income housing complex commonly known as, "the projects." Our household consisted of my mother and two younger sisters. My mom worked as a cleaning lady at a hospital for minimum wage. I remember money was always scarce. This prompted me as a young girl to find part-time work in the neighborhood such as babysitting and doing lawn work raking leaves. Needless to say, I never felt comfortable with lack. As a teenager, I worked at the community center and earned enough income to buy my own school clothes. This was a big help to my mom, who often struggled to financially provide for me and my sisters.

When school let out for summer break, we would spend the summer months with my aunt and uncle who lived in a nice suburban neighborhood. They owned real estate that generated rental income from their tenants allowing them a leisurely lifestyle. As property owners with cash flow, they could afford to take us to Disneyland or assist my mom with financial emergencies such as refrigerator repairs, a past-due utility bill, and other unexpected expenses.

From that point on, I knew what I wanted to become when I grew up: a property owner.

As children, we enjoyed our childhood. However, it was sometimes financially challenging for my mom, so as an adult, I was determined to make different choices, seize opportunities, and to learn to make smart money decisions.

After graduating high school and attending junior college, I was married, gave birth to my son, Brandon, and then divorced shortly thereafter. Fast forward a few years, I work from 9 to 5 at a telecommunications and media company. I have a good job with great benefits. I'm now a single mom in my late 20's. Brandon is at daycare during my work hours. We have a two-bedroom apartment in close proximity to my job and his daycare.

As a wage earner, I spend less than I earn. In other words, my living expenses are less than my net income from my paycheck, which allows me money left over for savings, emergencies, life insurance, and investing. I control my spending and credit charges. I review and revise my spending plan often, especially when considering future financial transactions.

START WHERE YOU ARE

My journey to next level abundance began when my landlord increased the monthly rent payment by $125 on my two-bedroom apartment. This prompted me to review my spending plan. To save $125 a month, I decided to move from the two-bedroom to a one-bedroom apartment. My son sleeps in the bedroom. I sleep on the sofa bed in the living room. When reviewing my spending plan, I also noticed I only have two more payments before my car is paid in full.

USE WHAT YOU HAVE

In two months, when my car is paid off, I'll have an additional $700 a month, $8,400 in twelve months, $16,800 in two years, and $25,200 in 36 months.

DO WHAT YOU CAN

I decided to redirect the funds from the monthly $700 car payment to use for my downpayment on rental income property.

From that time going forward, I would use what I have and do what I can to make owning income property my reality—using all the resources and opportunities available to me.

I will now share the strategies and consistent action steps taken to purchase rental income property.

FIRST THINGS FIRST

My first task was to prepare a Goal Setting Worksheet that clearly stated in detail the goal, mission, or objective I wanted to accomplish within a specific time frame or by a set date. Next, I developed strategies that describe how I intended to achieve my goal, mission, or objective. Lastly, I listed the step-by-step action steps or tasks to be completed to achieve each strategy.

The following is a summary or a short version of the Goal Setting Worksheet listing only the strategies for the stated goal. Note: The complete worksheet with goals, strategies, and action steps will be included in the next section.

My Objective: To purchase a multi-family (four-plex) income property that generates rental income.

Strategy

1. Start and continue a consistent savings for the four-plex down payment
2. Learn what specific due diligence is necessary to qualify for a mortgage loan to purchase a four-plex as residential income property.
3. Compile information regarding possible operating expenses to be considered for a four-plex income property.
4. Locate available rental properties for sale.
5. Determine if the income property is "profitable."
6. Research the fees and expenses included in the closing costs.
7. Obtain information regarding the closing process and complete each task to finalize the purchase of a four-plex rental property.

GOAL SETTING WORKSHEET

Objective, Mission, Goal

The goal, mission, or objective is to purchase income property that generates monthly rental income, specifically a four-plex that consists of four separate residential units within a single building, each with its own entrance, providing housing for four separate households, including a rent-free two-bedroom apartment for me and my son.

Strategy #1: Start and continue consistent savings for the four-plex down payment

Action Steps to be Completed:

1. Thirty days after the last car payment is made, schedule an appointment at the bank to open a new savings account entitled "Four-Plex Downpayment Savings Account."

   Date Task Completed: ______________

2. Make arrangements with the bank to authorize and schedule the automatic transfer of funds from my checking account to the new savings account in the amount of $[700.00] every month on or before the 17th of the month.

   Date Task Completed: ______________

3. Prepare a Deposit Chart that gives me a visual projection reflecting the monthly growth of my savings account over time.

   Date Task Completed: ______________

Former car payment		**Four-Plex Downpayment Savings Account**		
		Month	Deposit Amount	Savings Account Balance
$700		1	$700	$700
$700		2	$700	$1400
$700		3	$700	$2100
$700		4	$700	$2800
$700		5	$700	$3500
$700		6	$700	$4200
$700		7	$700	$4900
$700		8	$700	$5600
$700		9	$700	$6300
$700		10	$700	$7000
$700		11	$700	$7700
$700		12	$700	$8400
$700		**24**	$700	**$16,800**
$700		**36**	$700	**$25,200**

Strategy #2: Learn what due diligence is necessary to qualify for a mortgage loan to purchase a four-plex as a residential income property.

Action Steps to be Completed:

1. Ensure your credit score is strong, typically 620 or higher, as lenders use this to assess your creditworthiness.

2. Continue saving for the down payment, typically at least 20% of the purchase price for investment properties, though some programs may allow lower down payments, i.e., FHA allows a 3.5% downpayment.

3. Provide estimates of the rental income from the property, as some lenders may consider this income when evaluating your loan application.

   When financing a residential income property, lenders typically include a portion of the rental income from the tenants as part of the buyer's income. This is known as using the property's projected or actual rental income to help qualify for the loan.

   Here's how it generally works:
   Rental Income Calculation: Lenders usually consider about 75% of the gross rental income from the property to account for potential vacancies and maintenance costs. For instance, if the total rental income from the four-plex is $4,000 per month, the lender might consider $3,000 (75% of $4,000) as additional income for the buyer. The additional rental income can improve the buyer's debt-to-income ratio, making it easier to qualify for the loan.
   Documentation: The buyer may need to provide documentation of the rental income. This could include current lease agreements, rent rolls, and sometimes a history of rental income if the property is already occupied. For new purchases, a lender might require an appraisal with a rental income analysis.

Vacancy and Maintenance Factors: Lenders take into account the possibility of vacancies and maintenance costs, which is why they typically use 75% of the rental income rather than the full amount.

Note: It's always a good idea to consult with a mortgage broker or lender to understand the specific requirements and how rental income from a four-plex can be factored into your loan application.

4. Review your financial status, including income, debts, and assets. Lenders will scrutinize your debt-to-income (DTI) ratio, aiming for a DTI below 43%.

   Lenders use the debt-to-income ratio to determine what portion or percentage of your monthly income goes towards paying off monthly debts. The DTI ratio compares monthly debt obligations to gross monthly income.
   To calculate your debt-to-income (DTI) ratio, first determine your total monthly debt payments, which include obligations such as mortgage or rent, car loans, student loans, credit card minimum payments, and any other recurring debts. Next, calculate your gross monthly income, which is your total income before taxes and deductions, including salary, bonuses, and rental income. Divide your total monthly debt payments by your gross monthly income and multiply the result by 100 to convert it into a percentage. This percentage represents the portion of your income that goes towards paying off your debts and is a key indicator of your financial health and borrowing capacity. For example, if your total monthly debt payments are $1,500 and your gross monthly income is $5,000, your DTI ratio would be 30%, meaning that 30% of your income is allocated to debt repayments. Ideally, the DTI ratio should be below 43%, though some lenders may allow for higher ratios, especially if rental income from the four-plex is included.

5. Collect necessary documentation, such as tax returns, pay stubs, bank statements, proof of rental income, and details of existing debts and assets.
6. Get pre-approved for a mortgage to understand how much you can borrow and demonstrate your seriousness to sellers.
7. Research and explore different loan options, including conventional loans, FHA loans (if you plan to live in one of the units), and VA loans (if you qualify).

   Federal Housing Administration (FHA) loans are primarily aimed at helping individuals buy primary residences, but they can also be used to purchase rental properties under certain conditions.

   Features of FHA loans include lower credit score and down payment requirements, generally lower interest rates, mortgage insurance required for the life of the loan if less than 10% down, higher debt-to-income ratios allowed, and strict property standards. FHA loans can be assumed by a new buyer. An assumable mortgage loan allows a homebuyer to take over the seller's existing loan, typically under the same terms, which can be advantageous if the original loan has a lower interest rate than current market rates.

   Conventional Mortgage Loans require a higher credit score, and down payment requirements, potentially higher interest rates depending on financial profile, and mortgage insurance can be canceled once the Loan-to-Value (LTV) ratio reaches 80%, lower debt-to-income ratios, more flexibility in property conditions, typically not assumable, can be used for various types of properties.

   A VA mortgage loan offers benefits such as no down payment, competitive interest rates, and no private mortgage insurance (PMI) requirements, making homeownership more accessible and affordable for eligible veterans and active-duty service members.

8. The lender will require a professional appraisal of the property to determine its market value and ensure it meets loan requirements.
9. Arrange for a thorough inspection of the property to identify any potential issues or repairs needed.
10. Complete and submit your mortgage application along with all required documentation.
11. The lender will review your application, conduct a credit check, and verify all provided information during the underwriting process.
12. Once approved, review the loan terms, complete any remaining paperwork, and proceed to the closing process to finalize the purchase.

By following these procedures, you can better prepare yourself to qualify for a mortgage loan to purchase a four-plex rental property.

Summary: Schedule Time to Research and Learn Real Estate Principles and Terminology.

Make sure you have a thorough understanding of the following: Department of Housing and Urban Development (HUD) guidelines, private mortgage insurance, Fannie Mae and Freddie Mac, loan limits, interest rates, the pre-approval process, prepaids, points, loan terms; occupancy requirement; the underwriting process.

Strategy #3: Compile information regarding possible operating expenses to be considered for a four-plex income property.

Task: <u>Schedule Time to Research, Read, Study, Learn, and Review</u>

1. Property Management Fees
    - If you hire a property management company, expect to pay 8-12% of the monthly rental income.
2. Maintenance and Repairs
    - Regular maintenance (e.g., lawn care, snow removal) and unexpected repairs.
    - Budget about 1-3% of the property value annually for maintenance.
3. Utilities
    - Water, sewer, gas, electricity, and trash removal.
    - Costs may vary depending on whether tenants pay for their own utilities or if it's included in the rent.
4. Property Taxes
    - Varies by location; check local tax assessments.
    - Can be a significant expense; ensure you factor in the accurate amount.
5. Insurance
    - Property insurance to cover the building and liability insurance.
    - Typically costs around 0.25-0.5% of the property value annually.
6. Mortgage Payments
    - Principal and interest payments on any loan used to finance the property.
    - This is not an operating expense per se but an important consideration in overall cash flow.

7. Advertising and Leasing Fees

- Costs associated with marketing the property and finding new tenants.
- Leasing fees may apply if using a property management service.

8. Legal and Accounting Fees

- Costs for legal services (e.g., evictions) and accounting services for managing finances and taxes.

9. Landscaping and Lawn Care

- Regular upkeep of outdoor areas.
- Costs depend on the size of the property and the extent of landscaping.

10. Pest Control

- Regular pest control services to prevent infestations.

11. HOA Fees

- If the property is part of a homeowners' association, there may be monthly or annual fees.

12. Reserves for Replacements

- Setting aside funds for future capital expenditures like roof replacement, HVAC systems, and other major repairs.
- A common practice is to save 5-10% of rental income annually.

13. Vacancy and Collection Losses

- Income lost due to vacant units or non-paying tenants.
- Typically estimated at 5-10% of potential rental income.

Sample Budget Breakdown

Assuming a four-plex with a total annual rental income of $60,000, here is a sample budget:

Expense Category	Estimated Annual Cost
Property Management (10%)	$6,000
Maintenance and Repairs	$1,200 - $3,600
Utilities	$3,000
Property Taxes	$4,500
Insurance	$1,500
Advertising and Leasing	$500
Legal and Accounting	$1,000
Landscaping and Lawn Care	$1,200
Pest Control	$400
HOA Fees	N/A (if applicable)
Reserves for Replacements	$3,000
Vacancy and Collection Loss	$3,000 - $6,000

Total Estimated Annual Operating Expenses

- Low End: $24,300
- High End: $30,700

These estimates provide a general guideline, but actual costs can vary significantly. It's essential to perform a detailed analysis specific to your property and market conditions.

Strategy #4: Locate available rental properties for sale.

Action Steps to be Completed:

1. Define Your Criteria: Determine your investment goals, budget, preferred location, desired property condition, and other criteria to narrow your search.

2. Work with a Real Estate Agent: Partner with a real estate agent who specializes in multi-family and investment properties. They can provide access to listings, market insights, and professional guidance throughout the process.

3. Online Listings: Utilize online real estate platforms like Zillow, Realtor.com, Redfin, and LoopNet to search for four-plex properties. Set up alerts for new listings that meet your criteria.

4. Local MLS (Multiple Listing Service): Access the local MLS through your real estate agent to find comprehensive and up-to-date listings of four-plex properties in your desired area.

5. Real Estate Investment Groups: Join local real estate investment groups or associations. These groups often share information about available properties and can provide valuable networking opportunities.

6. Real Estate Auctions: Keep an eye on real estate auctions, where you might find four-plex properties for sale. Be sure to understand the auction process and potential risks involved.

7. Direct Mail Campaigns: Send direct mail letters to owners of four-plex properties in your target area expressing your interest in

purchasing their property. This approach can uncover off-market opportunities.

8. Networking: Network with other real estate investors, property managers, and real estate professionals who may have knowledge of four-plex properties for sale or upcoming listings.
9. Local Newspapers and Classifieds: Check local newspapers and online classified ads for listings of four-plex properties for sale.
10. Driving for Dollars: Drive through neighborhoods where you're interested in buying a four-plex. Look for "For Sale" signs and note any properties that appear vacant or in need of repair. You can contact the owners directly.
11. Social Media and Online Forums: Use social media platforms and online forums dedicated to real estate investing. Post your interest in buying a four-plex and connect with sellers or other investors.
12. Public Records: Search public records for properties with absentee owners or properties in foreclosure. These can be potential opportunities for purchasing a four-plex.

By following these procedures, you can effectively locate four-plex income properties for sale and find a suitable investment that meets your needs and goals.

Strategy #5: Determine if the rental property is "profitable". In other words, (a) is the property's monthly rent at least 1% of the purchase price to be considered a potentially profitable investment; (b) does the property generate positive cash flow; (c) does the property's rental income cover the mortgage payments; and (d) what is the return on investment that indicates the rental property is potentially profitable.

Task: Schedule Time to Research, Read, Study, Learn, Review

a. The 1% rule is a guideline used by real estate investors to quickly evaluate whether a rental property is likely to generate sufficient cash flow and be a good investment. According to the 1% rule, the monthly rent of an income property should be at least 1% of the property's purchase price (including any initial renovation costs) to be considered a potentially profitable investment.

For example: If a property is purchased for $200,000, then according to the 1% rule, it should generate at least $2,000 per month in rent ($200,000 × 0.01 = $2,000)

b. A rental property is profitable when the property generates positive cash flow. Cash flow in rental income property refers to the amount of money left over after all expenses related to the property have been paid. This includes mortgage payments, property taxes, insurance, maintenance, and any other costs associated with the property. Positive cash flow occurs when the rental income exceeds these expenses, providing a steady income stream for the property owner. Managing and maximizing cash flow is crucial for the long-term success and profitability of rental investments.

To determine if a rental property has positive cash flow, you start by calculating the Gross Monthly Rental Income, which is the total income generated from rent each month. Next, subtract the Monthly Operating Expenses, which include costs such as property management fees, maintenance, utilities, property taxes, insurance, and any reserves for vacancies. This gives you the Net Operating Income (NOI). From the NOI, subtract the Monthly Debt Payments, which primarily include the mortgage payments (principal and interest) and any other loans associated with the property. If the resulting figure is positive, the property has positive cash flow, meaning it generates more income than it costs to operate and finance. This positive cash flow is crucial for maintaining the property's profitability and ensuring a steady return on investment.

c. A rental property is profitable when the property's rental income covers the mortgage payments.

There is a self-sufficiency test requirement for FHA loans when purchasing a multi-family property (such as a duplex, triplex, or four-plex). The self-sufficiency test is designed to ensure that the property's rental income is sufficient to cover the mortgage payments. Here's how it works:

<u>Self-Sufficiency Test Requirements</u>

1. Gross Rental Income Calculation:

   Calculate the total gross rental income from all units, including the unit that the borrower will occupy. This is usually done using either current lease agreements or, if the property is not fully rented, an appraiser's estimate of fair market rents.

2. 75% Rule:

   The lender will use 75% of the gross rental income for the self-sufficiency test to account for vacancies and maintenance costs. For example, if the total gross rental income is $4,000 per month, the lender will consider $3,000 (75% of $4,000) as the qualifying rental income.

3. Monthly Mortgage Payment Comparison:

   The qualifying rental income (75% of gross rental income) must be equal to or greater than the total monthly mortgage payment, which includes principal, interest, taxes, insurance, and any homeowners' association (HOA) fees, if applicable.

Example

- Total Gross Rental Income: $4,000 per month
- Qualifying Rental Income (75%): $3,000 per month
- Total Monthly Mortgage Payment: $2,800 per month

In this example, the qualifying rental income ($3,000) is greater than the total monthly mortgage payment ($2,800), so the property would pass the self-sufficiency test.

Purpose of the Test

The self-sufficiency test ensures that the property can generate enough income to cover its own expenses, reducing the risk to both the borrower and the lender. This requirement is particularly important for FHA loans, as they have lower down payment requirements and are backed by the government.

Exceptions and Considerations

- Single-Family Homes: The self-sufficiency test does not apply to single-family homes or properties with only one unit.
- Lender Requirements: While the FHA sets the basic guidelines, individual lenders may have additional requirements or stricter criteria.
- Documentation: Proper documentation of rental income, such as leases and rental income estimates from an appraiser, is essential.

It's important to consult with an FHA-approved lender to understand the specific requirements and how they apply to your situation. They can provide detailed guidance on the self-sufficiency test and help you determine if a property meets the criteria.

d. The capitalization rate, or cap rate, is crucial when acquiring rental properties because it provides a quick and straightforward way to assess the potential return on investment (ROI) and profitability relative to its market value or purchase price. Specifically, the cap rate reflects the ratio of the property's Net Operating Income (NOI) to its current market value or purchase price, expressed as a percentage. The cap rate represents the percentage of the property's value that the investor can expect to earn annually from the property's operating income, excluding financing costs. For example, a 6% cap rate means the investor can expect a 6% return on the property's value each year from rental income. The capitalization rate (cap rate) has a direct impact on the purchase price of a rental property because it is used to assess the property's value based on its income-generating potential.

Here's how the cap rate indicates profitability:

1. High Cap Rate: A higher cap rate suggests that the property generates more income relative to its value, indicating higher profitability. However, it can also imply higher risk, such as being in a less desirable location or having more volatile income streams.

2. Low Cap Rate: A lower cap rate indicates lower returns relative to the property's value, which might suggest lower profitability. Properties with lower cap rates are often in more stable, desirable locations and are considered lower risk, but the income return may be less attractive.

   Example:

   - NOI: $50,000
   - Property Value: $1,000,000
   - Cap Rate: 5%

In this example, the property's annual return is 5% of its value. Investors typically compare this rate to other investment opportunities and their risk tolerance. A cap rate that aligns with or exceeds an investor's required return threshold indicates that the rental property is potentially profitable. However, the cap rate should be evaluated alongside other factors such as property condition, market trends, and long-term appreciation potential to get a comprehensive view of profitability.

Strategy #6: Research the fees and expenses included in the closing costs.

Task: Schedule Time to Research, Read, Study, Learn, Review

There are closing costs associated with FHA loans for purchasing rental property, just as there are with any other type of mortgage. These costs typically include various fees and expenses that are paid at the closing of the mortgage transaction. Here's a breakdown of common closing costs for FHA loans:

<u>Common Closing Costs for FHA Loans</u>

1. <u>Loan Origination Fee</u>

   This is a fee charged by the lender for processing the loan. It is usually a percentage of the loan amount, often around 1%.

2. <u>Appraisal Fee</u>

   An FHA-approved appraiser must appraise the property to determine its value and ensure it meets FHA standards. The fee typically ranges from $300 to $500 but can be higher depending on the property's location and complexity.

3. <u>Credit Report Fee</u>

   The lender will check your credit report as part of the loan application process. This fee is usually around $30 to $50.

4. Title Insurance

   Title insurance protects against potential issues with the property's title. Both lender's and owner's title insurance policies are required, with costs varying based on the property value and location.

5. Escrow Fees

   Escrow or closing fees are charged by the title company or escrow company for managing the closing process. These fees can range from a few hundred to over a thousand dollars.

6. Recording Fees

   These are fees for recording the mortgage and deed with the county or municipality. The cost varies by location but is usually a few hundred dollars.

7. Prepaid Expenses

   - Homeowners Insurance: Lenders typically require a year's worth of homeowners insurance to be paid at closing.
   - Property Taxes: A few months' worth of property taxes may be collected at closing.
   - Mortgage Insurance Premium (MIP): FHA loans require an upfront MIP of 1.75% of the loan amount, which can be rolled into the loan. Additionally, an annual MIP is divided into monthly payments.

8. Flood Certification Fee

   This fee, usually around $20, determines whether the property is located in a flood zone and requires flood insurance.

9. Survey Fee

   In some cases, a survey of the property may be required to confirm property boundaries. This fee can range from $300 to $600.

10. Attorney Fees

    In some states, an attorney's involvement is required for the closing. Fees vary widely based on location and complexity.

Total Closing Costs

The total closing costs for an FHA loan typically range from 2% to 5% of the loan amount. For example, on a $200,000 loan, closing costs might range from $4,000 to $10,000.

Closing Cost Assistance

1. Seller Contributions or Seller Concessions: FHA rules allow sellers to contribute up to 6% of the purchase price toward the buyer's closing costs. Seller concessions in real estate refer to the costs that the seller agrees to cover on behalf of the buyer, such as closing costs, home inspections, or repairs, which can make the purchase more affordable for the buyer by reducing the amount of cash they need to bring to the closing table.

   Gift Funds: Borrowers can use gift funds from family members or other approved sources to cover closing costs.

2. Lender Credits: Some lenders offer credits towards closing costs in exchange for a higher interest rate.

Summary

Closing costs are an important consideration when purchasing a rental property with an FHA loan. Understanding these costs and exploring potential assistance options can help you better prepare for the financial aspects of the transaction.

Strategy #7: Obtain information regarding the closing process and complete each task to finalize the purchase of a four-plex rental property.

Action Steps to be Completed:

1. Final Walk-Through: Conduct a final walk-through of the property to ensure it is in the agreed-upon condition and that any requested repairs have been completed.

2. Review Closing Disclosure: Receive and review the Closing Disclosure at least three business days before closing. This document outlines the final loan terms, monthly payments, fees, and other costs.

3. Obtain Homeowners Insurance: Purchase homeowner's insurance and provide proof of coverage to your lender. This is typically required before the closing can occur.

4. Secure Funds for Closing: Arrange for the necessary funds to cover the down payment, closing costs, and any other required payments. These funds should be in the form of a certified check or wire transfer.

5. Title Search and Insurance: Ensure a title search has been completed to verify the property's ownership history and to check for any liens or encumbrances. Purchase title insurance to protect against future claims.

6. Final Loan Approval: Complete any final requirements from the lender for loan approval, which may include providing additional documentation or clarifications.

7. Signing Documents: Attend the closing meeting, typically held at a title company, attorney's office, or escrow office. Sign all necessary documents, including the mortgage note, deed of trust, and other loan and property-related paperwork.

8. Pay Closing Costs: Pay all closing costs, which may include loan origination fees, appraisal fees, title insurance, escrow fees, and other related expenses.

9. Record Deed: The signed deed and other documents will be recorded with the appropriate government office to officially transfer ownership of the property to you.

10. Receive Keys: Once all documents are signed and funds are transferred, you will receive the keys to the property and take possession.

11. Post-Closing Activities: After closing, ensure all utilities are transferred to your name, update your address with relevant institutions, and begin managing your new four-plex rental property.

By following these steps, you can successfully complete the closing process and finalize the purchase of your four-plex income property.

DO WHAT YOU CAN:

Every week diligently schedule time to research, read, study, learn, and review:

- The types of mortgage loans commonly available to first-time homebuyers. [Strategy #2]
- the possible operating expenses to be considered for an income property. [Strategy #3]
- the fees and expenses included in the closing costs. [Strategy #6]
- the procedures pertaining to the closing process [Strategy #7]

Get ready and be ready to provide the following information or submit documentation to the mortgage lender:

- Proof of a strong credit score; documentation regarding income, debts, and assets; evidence of downpayment; financial records such as tax returns, pay stubs, and bank statements; estimates of the rental income from the property; property report from a professional appraiser to determine the property's market value; an inspection report to address any potential repairs needed; mortgage application completed and returned. [Strategy 2]

Action steps to be completed by YOU, the buyer:

- Start and continue consistent savings for the four-plex down-payment. [Strategy #1]
- Locate a four-plex income property for sale. [Strategy #4]
- Determine if the income property is "profitable." [Strategy #5]
- Set aside funds to cover the fees and expenses included in the closing costs. [Strategy #6]
- Get pre-approved for a mortgage. [Strategy 2]
- Research and explore different loan options. [Strategy #2]
- Complete each applicable task pertaining to the closing process. [Strategy #7]
- Review the loan terms, and complete any remaining paperwork once the loan is approved. [Strategy #2]

NICOLE'S PERSONAL JOURNEY TO NEXT LEVEL ABUNDANCE

Total Amount Saved. Within three years, Nicole was able to save $25,200 for the downpayment and closing cost.

Downpayment Savings Account		$25,200.00
Down payment	$ 8,750.00	
Closing Cost	+ 9,221.88	

Sub-Total	$17,971.88	- $17,971.88
Saving Account Balance/Reserves*		$7,228.12

*Reserves: Some lenders might also require reserves equal to several months' worth of principal, interest, taxes, and insurance (PITI), as well as reserves (savings) to cover a few months of mortgage payments.

<u>List Price of the Property, Down Payment</u>. While in the process of saving for the downpayment, earnest deposit, and closing costs, Nicole located a four-plex rental property with a list price of $250,000. The down payment required for an FHA loan is 3.5% of the purchase price, as she and her son intend to live in one of the units. The downpayment is $8,750 ($250,000 times .0350).

<u>Interest Rate; Loan Term, Monthly Mortgage Payment</u>. Her monthly mortgage payment, with a 5.25% interest rate and a 30-year loan term, would be approximately $1,332.19. This calculation does not include property taxes, homeowner's insurance, or mortgage insurance premiums (MIP), which are typically required for FHA loans and can affect the total monthly payment.

<u>Closing Costs</u>. So, the approximate closing costs for a multi-family FHA property with a 3.5% down payment, a list price of $250,000, and a 5.25% interest rate for a 30-year term would be between $9,221.88 and $16,721.88. For a property with a list price of $250,000, she can expect closing costs to be in this range.

<u>CONCLUSION:</u> CHAPTER 3 (OPPORTUNITY TO LEVEL UP)

As you can see from Nicole's Goal Setting Worksheet, problems are solved when your intentions and actions are in alignment.

Throughout this journey, Nicole applied specific tools to get her desired results – tools such as developing a next-level mindset and establishing income-producing habits, i.e., researching, reading, learning, following through, and discipline. She practiced the art of dreaming big and thinking big to expand her vision into a reality. By embracing opportunities, she was able to achieve a significant milestone – becoming a real estate investor, property owner, and landlord.

The Goal Setting Worksheet provided step-by-step solutions to get Nicole from a rented one-bedroom apartment, sleeping on the sofa bed in the living room, to owning a multi-family (four-plex) income property with one of the four apartments reserved for Nicole and her son as the new owners.

CHAPTER 4:
HEAD START OPPORTUNITIES

Head start opportunities in connection with personal finances mean starting to save or invest at a younger age or building good financial habits early on. By doing so, you give yourself more time to grow wealth, take advantage of compound interest, and reach your financial goals ahead of others who may start later. Essentially, it's about getting ahead of the curve to improve long-term financial outcomes, as characterized here by David and his family.

David is 35 years old, married to his wife Regina who works as a legal secretary. They have two children: a son, Kevin, who is 5 years old, and their daughter, Christine, age two. David's family origin consists of his mother, father, two siblings, a brother and sister, and a cousin named Nicole. Both of David's siblings, James and Cathy have one child each. His cousin Nicole has one son.

Hi, my name is David. I began my career fifteen years ago as an accounting clerk. I work at a Chicago-based corporation in the stock transfer department. The company I work for is a publicly traded company in the automobile manufacturing industry. A publicly traded company means that anyone can buy or sell ownership stakes, known as "shares," in the company. Owning shares in a publicly traded company means that you own a small portion of that company.

Shares, also known as stocks or equity, represent a fractional ownership interest in the company. When you buy shares, you become a shareholder, which entitles you to certain rights depending on the number of shares you own.

$ $

As I stated earlier, I work in the stock transfer department.

The Stock Transfer Department is responsible for managing and overseeing the accurate transfer of stock ownership within a company. Its primary functions include maintaining the shareholder register, ensuring that all transactions—such as stock purchases, sales, and transfers—are correctly recorded, and issuing or canceling stock certificates as needed. Additionally, the department manages dividend distributions, handles shareholder inquiries, and ensures compliance with relevant securities laws and regulations. By facilitating smooth and secure stock transactions and maintaining accurate records, the Stock Transfer Department plays a vital role in supporting shareholder relations and ensuring the company's adherence to legal and regulatory requirements.

Several years ago, I was promoted from accounting clerk to stock transfer analyst. I'm responsible for processing the transfer of stock ownership between parties. This includes verifying the authenticity of transfer requests, ensuring proper documentation is provided, and updating shareholder records to reflect the new ownership. I also ensure that the company's shareholder register is accurate and up to date. This involves recording new shareholders, updating existing records, and managing any changes in shareholder information. My duties also include the preparation, issuance, and cancellation of stock certificates ensuring that certificates are accurately produced and securely delivered to shareholders.

Over the years, while working as a stock transfer analyst, I've noticed a vast number of the company's stock is owned by young children. In many of these situations, the parents and grandparents who already own stock will transfer a percentage of shares to the children.

REACHING FINANCIAL GOALS EARLY IN LIFE

Sample Scenario: let's say Grandpa Jones currently owns 500 shares of XYZ Corp and wants to transfer 20% (100 shares) to his three-year-old granddaughter, Lisa.

Grandpa Jones:

- Completes a stock transfer form authorizing the transfer of 100 shares to Lisa, his granddaughter.
- Submits the stock transfer form and any existing stock certificate to the transfer agent.
- The transfer agent cancels the original stock certificate, issuing a new certificate for 400 shares to Grandpa Jones, the original owner, and another certificate for 100 shares to Lisa, the new owner.

Both Grandpa Jones and Lisa will now hold shares based on the transferred percentage.

Instead of birthday or Christmas gifts, many children receive additional shares of the company's stock year after year to grow their financial portfolio. This observation led me to think, *"These children's parents and grandparents are making smart money decisions on their behalf, ensuring the children are starting off with a strong financial foundation. Their children and grandchildren are shareholders with investments that are growing and multiplying in value year after year. When they become adults, they will receive investment income from their stock in the company that will enable them to live very lavish lifestyles."*

Since most of the adults in our family don't currently own stock to transfer or pass down to the next generation, this prompted me to research other investment options that focus on growing wealth.

GROWTH SECURITIES FOR THE CHILDREN AS LONG-TERM INVESTORS

Growth securities are financial instruments, typically stocks, representing companies that are expected to experience high revenue and profit growth. Rather than paying dividends, companies issuing growth securities focus on expanding the business, increasing revenue, and potentially delivering substantial capital gains to investors over time. Capital gains refer to the profit made when an asset (stock) is sold for more than its purchase price.

Growth Mutual Funds

A mutual fund is a type of investment that pools money from many people to buy a mix of stocks, bonds, or other assets. It is managed by a professional fund manager who decides where to invest the money to meet specific goals, such as growth, income, or safety. Investors buy shares in the mutual fund, and the value of their shares changes based on the performance of the fund's investments. It's an easy way for people to diversify their investments without having to pick individual stocks or manage the portfolio themselves.

Growth Mutual Funds are funds that invest primarily in growth stocks. Examples include funds that track indices like the S&P 500 Growth Index, DJIA, or the NASDAQ 100.

The S&P 500 ("Standard & Poor") is a stock market index that tracks the performance of 500 of the largest publicly traded companies in the United States. The index is also known for its strong historical returns, making it an attractive option for long-term investors. Because it represents a broad cross-section of the U.S. economy, investing in the S&P 500 provides exposure to some of the most stable and successful companies, offering growth potential with relatively lower risk.

DJIA stands for the Dow Jones Industrial Average. It is a stock market index that tracks the performance of 30 large, publicly traded blue-chip companies in the United States. Blue chip companies are large, well-established, and financially stable businesses with a history of reliable performance over time. Examples of blue-chip companies include Apple, Microsoft, Coca-Cola, and Johnson & Johnson. They are considered safe, long-term investments due to their proven track records, solid financials, and ability to weather market fluctuations.

Diversification: Both indices represent a broad range of large, well-established companies across various industries. Companies in the index represent various sectors, including technology, finance, healthcare, and consumer goods, providing investors with diversified exposure to different sectors without the need to buy individual stocks.

The NASDAQ 100 is a stock market index that tracks the performance of 100 of the largest non-financial companies listed on the NASDAQ stock exchange. It is heavily weighted toward technology and innovation-driven sectors, including companies like Apple, Microsoft, and Tesla, but also includes firms in healthcare, consumer goods, and telecommunications. The full name of NASDAQ is the National Association of Securities Dealers Automated Quotations.

OPENING AN INVESTMENT ACCOUNT FOR MINOR CHILDREN

It's important to position our children and grandchildren to own income-producing assets as shareholders beginning NOW – rather than later when they become adults. This is known as a Head Start Opportunity.

Minor children (under the age of 18) can become shareholders, typically through custodial accounts. A custodial account is a financial account managed by an adult (often a parent or guardian) on behalf of a minor, allowing the adult to purchase, hold, and retain ownership of stock or other investments for the child until the child reaches the age of majority (typically 18 or 21, depending on the state). When an investor "holds" a stock, they choose to keep it in their portfolio, believing that it will continue to generate returns in the future through price appreciation, dividends, or both. To generate returns refers to the profit or income an investor earns from their investment.

While minors cannot directly own stock or vote at shareholder meetings, their shares still entitle them to dividends and potential capital gains. Capital gains in connection with stocks refer to the profit an investor earns when they sell a stock for more than they originally paid for it. This increase in the stock's value over time represents the capital gain, and it can be realized when the stock is sold. Capital gains are typically subject to taxation, with rates varying depending on how long the stock was held before being sold (short-term or long-term capital gains).

The Uniform Gifts to Minors Act ("UGMA") is a law that allows minors to own assets through custodial accounts. UGMA accounts are often used by parents, grandparents, or other adults to gift money or securities to a minor without setting up a formal trust. This can be a great way to introduce children to investing and help build wealth for their future. However, because minors cannot make legal decisions, the custodian has the responsibility to act in the best interest of the child until they are legally able to take control of the account.

Custodial accounts are typically opened at brokerage firms. A brokerage firm is a financial institution that facilitates the buying and selling of securities, such as stocks, bonds, and mutual funds, on behalf of individual and institutional investors.

A brokerage account for minors, often set up as a custodial account, allows an adult to manage investments, such as stocks, on behalf of a child. The account is held in the child's name, and all assets within it legally belong to the minor, though the adult makes the investment decisions until the child reaches the age of majority. Once the child is of age, they gain full control over the brokerage account and can make their own investment choices. This type of account can be a great way to build wealth and introduce financial education to children early on.

$ $

Uniform Gifts to Minors Act

Key Points of UGMA Custodial Accounts:

- A custodial account is created at a brokerage firm in the name of the minor, but a designated custodian (usually an adult) manages the assets in the account until the minor reaches the age of majority.
- The assets in a UGMA account legally belong to the minor. The custodian manages the account but must use the assets for the benefit of the child.
- UGMA accounts primarily allow for the transfer of financial assets like cash, stocks, and bonds.
- Once the money or securities are placed into the UGMA account, they are considered irrevocable gifts to the minor and cannot be taken back by the custodian or the donor.
- Earnings in UGMA accounts are taxed at the child's tax rate, which may be lower than the adult's tax rate. However, there are certain tax thresholds known as the "kiddie tax," which, if exceeded, may cause some earnings to be taxed at the adult's rate.
- The custodian controls the account until the minor reaches the age of majority, at which point the minor gains full control over the assets.

$ $

David continues

At this point, after completing my research regarding investment principles and procedures, I scheduled a family meeting to share the information I learned and to discuss each parent starting custodial investment accounts for the children in our family, which includes my two children, my nieces, and nephews as well as my cousin's child.

The purpose of the family meeting was to discuss the financial future of our children. During the meeting, we had the following question and answer session:

<u>Q&A TO DISCUSS THE CHILDREN BECOMING INVESTORS</u>.

<u>Question</u>: Since our children are very young and we are getting a head start with financial literacy, what type of investments are recommended for wealth accumulation?

<u>Answer</u>: Investors who prioritize long-term growth over immediate income often see greater increases in their net worth from growth mutual funds. These investments are typically best suited for wealth building over the long haul, potentially resulting in substantial wealth accumulation for patient investors who have time to allow investments to multiply and grow.

<u>Question</u>: How does investing in growth mutual funds on behalf of our children benefit them and increase their net worth as investors?

<u>Answer</u>: Growth mutual funds are an excellent tool for wealth accumulation, especially for long-term investors. They focus on investing in companies with strong potential for capital appreciation. Capital appreciation increases net worth as the value of the growth stocks increases over time. By reinvesting earnings and capital gains, these funds leverage the power of compounding, allowing investments to grow faster. Additionally, growth mutual funds provide diversification by spreading investments across multiple high-growth companies and sectors, which helps reduce the overall risk. Their potential for significant long-term gains makes them ideal for building wealth and achieving financial goals.

Question: How do growth mutual funds differ from dividend-paying stocks?

Answer: The primary difference between growth mutual funds and income-producing assets, like dividend-paying stocks, lies in their investment goals. Growth mutual funds, such as stocks in fast-growing companies, aim to increase in value over time, providing returns primarily through capital appreciation rather than regular payouts. In contrast, income-producing assets, like dividend-paying stock, focus on providing a steady stream of regular income through dividends or interest payments.

Unlike income-producing assets that prioritize regular payouts, growth mutual funds prioritize increasing the value of the investment, making them ideal for investors who can forgo short-term income in favor of larger gains in the future.

Question: What is the average investment requirement for beginner investors?

Answer: Many mutual funds have a minimum initial investment requirement, typically ranging from $500 to $3,000. Some funds targeted at beginner investors, like certain index mutual funds, may have lower minimums (around $100 to $500).

Question: What financial resources do we, parents, have available to start and fund each child's investment account?

Answer: The funds previously spent on discretionary expenses and unnecessary items can now be redirected and repurposed to fund the children's custodial investment accounts.

"WHAT IF" Scenarios to repurpose discretionary and non-essential expenses		
What if, you quit smoking cigarettes; [one pack a day at $8.00 a pack. By the end of the week, you would have $56; in two weeks $112; in one month $240; in one year $2920]		
Possible Amount to be Repurposed to Reduce or Pay Off Debts:		
Within 12 mos	Within 18 mos	Within 24 mos
$2920	$4320	$5840

Imagine this, the day has arrived, you've made your final car payment of $700 per month. Now is the time to make a smart money decision to redirect the $700 to reduce another debt or increase your savings.		
Possible Amount to be Repurposed to Reduce or Pay Off Debts:		
Within 12 mos	Within 18 mos	Within 24 mos
$8400	$12,600	$16,800

Your toddler is now potty-trained. Yay!!!!, The average cost for disposable diapers costing $75 per month is an expense you can transfer and redirect to another expense to reduce debts.		
Possible Amount to be Repurposed to Reduce or Pay Off Debts:		
Within 12 mos	Within 18 mos	Within 24 mos
$900	$1350	$1800

What if you limit your daily trips to your favorite coffee shop to every other day or four days a week. If your family's daily coffee shop order usually cost $19.00 that's a savings of $57 per week; $228 per month and $2736 a year when you limit your trips to the coffee shop to four times a week.		
Possible Amount to be Repurposed to Reduce or Pay Off Debts:		
Within 12 mos	Within 18 mos	Within 24 mos
$2736	$4104	$5472

Congratulations!!! Your child is graduating from daycare moving on to first grade in the public school district. For many parents, childcare costs approximately $800 a month. Once the child enters public school, this expense can be redirected to pay off or reduce another debt.		
Possible Amount to be Repurposed to Reduce or Pay Off Debts:		
Within 12 mos	Within 18 mos	Within 24 mos
$9600	$14,400	$19,200

<u>Question</u>: What are the initial procedures to open an investment account for the children?

<u>Answer</u>: Here are the Procedures for Opening a Custodial Account

1. <u>Choose the Type of Account</u>:

   UTMA vs. UGMA: UTMA (Uniform Transfers to Minors Act) accounts allow broader asset types (e.g., real estate), while UGMA accounts are limited to financial assets (e.g., stocks, bonds). Choose the right account based on the types of investments you plan to hold for the minor.

2. <u>Select a Custodian</u>:

   The custodian (usually a parent or guardian) is responsible for managing the account until the child reaches the age of majority. Ensure the custodian is willing and capable of managing the funds and making appropriate investment decisions.

3. <u>Choose a Brokerage Firm or Financial Institution</u>:

   Select a brokerage firm or financial institution that offers custodial accounts (e.g., Vanguard, Fidelity, Charles Schwab). Consider factors such as fees, investment options, account minimums, and ease of use.

4. <u>Complete an Application Form</u>

   Fill out the brokerage or bank's custodial account application form. This will require:

- **Personal information** for the custodian (name, address, Social Security Number, etc.).
- **Personal information** for the minor (name, address, Social Security Number, etc.).
- **Identification documents** for both the custodian and the minor (e.g., driver's license, passport, birth certificate).

5. Provide Social Security Numbers:

   Both the minor's and the custodian's Social Security numbers will be needed for tax reporting purposes.

6. Fund the Account:

   Deposit the initial funds into the custodial account. This can be done via:

   - Bank transfer
   - Check deposit
   - Transfer of existing securities (in some cases)

7. Choose Investments:

   Once the account is funded, the custodian can choose the types of investments (e.g., stocks, bonds, mutual funds, ETFs) that will be held in the account. Ensure that the investments align with the long-term financial goals for the minor.

8. Understand Tax Implications:

   Earnings from custodial accounts are subject to the "kiddie tax," meaning some of the income may be taxed at the parents' tax rate. Monitor tax liabilities, and consider consulting with a tax advisor to understand how gains, dividends, or interest will be taxed.

9. Comply with State Laws:

   The age at which the child assumes control of the account varies by state. Typically, this is 18 or 21, but it can differ based on local regulations. Ensure you comply with your state's laws regarding custodial accounts and the transfer of assets.

10. Monitor the Account:

   Regularly review the account's performance and ensure it is managed prudently. Be aware of the eventual transfer of control to the minor when they reach the age of majority.

Following these procedures will ensure that you can effectively open and manage a custodial account for a minor.

Question: How can we grow and multiply the custodial account once it has been opened?

Answer: These are the procedures to make regular deposits into a growth mutual fund account:

1. Open a Mutual Fund Account**.** If you haven't already, open an account with a brokerage or mutual fund company. Provide personal information, such as your name, address, Social Security Number, and banking details.

2. Link Your Bank Account to the Mutual Fund Account. Most mutual fund companies and brokerages allow you to link your bank account for automated transfers. You may need to provide your bank's routing number and your account number.

3. Set Up a Systematic Investment Plan (SIP). Many mutual fund companies offer a Systematic Investment Plan (SIP), allowing you to schedule regular monthly contributions. Choose the amount to be deposited each month and the date for the transfer.

4. Make Automatic Deposits. Authorize automatic transfers from your bank account to the mutual fund account. Ensure you have sufficient funds in your bank account to avoid overdrafts or failed transactions.

5. Monitor Your Investments. Regularly review your account statements to track your contributions and the performance of the mutual fund. Adjust the monthly deposit amount if your financial situation changes.

Tips for Success:

- Consistency: Automating deposits helps ensure consistent investing, which is key to long-term growth.
- Dollar-Cost Averaging: Monthly contributions allow you to take advantage of dollar-cost averaging, reducing the impact of market volatility.
- Reassess Goals: Periodically review your investment goals and the performance of your mutual fund to ensure it aligns with your financial objectives.

Question: Currently, my son is five years old. Let's say I make an initial investment of $500 to start his investment account, and I make monthly contributions of $200 or $100 every payday for the next 20 years. What would be the value of the investment account when my son is 25 years old?

Answer: The value of his investment account would be well over $100,000. This reflects the growth due to both your initial investment and the monthly contributions over time, assuming a 7% annual growth rate.

With an initial investment of $500 and monthly contributions of $200 for 20 years, the results are as follows:

- Total Future Value: $103,442.12
- Total Contributions: $48,500

- Capital Appreciation: $54,942.12

This demonstrates how increased monthly contributions significantly boost long-term growth due to compounding.

$ $

During this meeting, our family decided it is our intention to establish a family legacy, which includes building a strong financial foundation which is crucial for the family to prosper as a whole. It begins with establishing good financial habits, consistent savings, and profitable investments, which collectively ensure long-term financial health from generation to generation, starting with the young children in our family. This legacy will be built on prioritizing financial education and open discussions about money within the family. Each generation will be equipped with the knowledge and tools to sustain and enhance the family's wealth.

CONCLUSION: CHAPTER 4 (HEAD START OPPORTUNITY)

David's entire family seized an opportunity to work together, and share ideas, resources, and responsibilities to start, establish, and maintain the family's legacy, starting with the young children. The family's intention is to create a legacy starting here, starting now that will be passed down from this generation to the next generation.

Disclaimer from the author: The information provided herein is for educational and informational purposes only and should not be construed as financial, investment, or legal advice. Investing in securities, including stocks, mutual funds, ETFs, REITs, and bonds, carries inherent risks, including the potential loss of principal. Before making any investment decisions, readers and investors should conduct their own research, assess their risk tolerance, and consult with a qualified financial advisor or professional.

CHAPTER 5: OPPORTUNITY TO PROSPER

Now that the children have a financial head-start owning investments through their custodial brokerage accounts, it's time to focus on financial opportunities for the adult family members.

Opportunity to Prosper is the opportunity level for adults and families who are ready to prosper financially.

The word "opportunity" is defined as a set of circumstances that makes it possible to do something. The word "circumstances" means a fact or condition connected with or relevant to an event or action. The purpose of this book is to demonstrate to the reader that it is POSSIBLE to ACHIEVE next-level abundance with consistent ACTIONS. In other words, to achieve the intended outcome or to arrive at the desired destination, one must consistently act on opportunities when they are presented.

ARRIVING AT THE DESIRED DESTINATION

An itinerary is a detailed plan or schedule outlining the sequence of activities, events, or destinations for a trip or journey.

Travel Itinerary – Destination: Portland, Oregon

Imagine scheduling a trip to attend your best friend's wedding in Portland, Oregon. You're currently living in Shreveport, Louisiana. Upon receiving the travel itinerary, you notice you have several connecting flights to get to your destination.

Here's a sample itinerary with four connecting flights from Shreveport, Louisiana, to Portland, Oregon. This route involves multiple connections:

1st Flight:	From: Shreveport, LA	To: Dallas/Fort Worth, TX
2nd Flight:	From: Dallas/Fort Worth, TX	To: Denver, CO
3rd Flight:	From: Denver, CO	To: Seattle, WA
4th Flight	From: Seattle, WA	To: Portland

Connecting flights are often necessary to reach certain destinations, especially when flying from smaller regional airports to more commonly served locations.

$$$$$$$$$$$$$$$$$$$$$$$$$$$$$$$$

Financial Itinerary – Destination: An Abundant Lifestyle

As with multiple connecting flights, an abundant lifestyle often requires multiple sources of income to maneuver from one financial level to the next.

Here are examples of various income sources as options to level up financially step by step: Each level is intended to provide revenue to fund or finance the next level.

1st Level: Repurpose money spent on discretionary expenses

2nd Level: Start a home-based business

3rd Level: Produce multiple streams of residual income

4th Level Generate income-producing assets

$$$$$$$$$$$$$$$$$$$$$$$$$$$$$$$$

Options for Multiple Sources of Income

1st Level: Repurposing Money Spent on Discretionary Expenses

Opportunity: Free up money from your salary by eliminating or reducing discretionary or unnecessary expenses. This simple act will generate a surplus of money to fund the next level.

Here are a few ways to generate additional income by repurposing money from discretionary or unnecessary expenses.

"WHAT IF" Scenarios to repurpose discretionary and non-essential expenses		
What if, you quit smoking cigarettes; [one pack a day at $8.00 a pack. By the end of the week, you would have $56; in two weeks $112; in one month $240; in one year $2920]		
Possible Amount to be Repurposed to Reduce or Pay Off Debts:		
Within 12 mos	Within 18 mos	Within 24 mos
$2920	$4320	$5840

Imagine this, the day has arrived, you've made your final car payment of $700 per month. Now is the time to make a smart money decision to redirect the $700 to reduce another debt or increase your savings.		
Possible Amount to be Repurposed to Reduce or Pay Off Debts:		
Within 12 mos	Within 18 mos	Within 24 mos
$8400	$12,600	$16,800

Your toddler is now potty-trained. Yay!!!!, The average cost for disposable diapers costing $75 per month, is an expense you can transfer and redirect to another expense to reduce debts.		
Possible Amount to be Repurposed to Reduce or Pay Off Debts:		
Within 12 mos	Within 18 mos	Within 24 mos
$900	$1350	$1800

What if you limit your daily trips to your favorite coffee shop to every other day or four days a week. If your family's daily coffee shop order usually cost $19.00 that's a savings of $57 per week; $228 per month, and $2736 a year when you limit your trips to the coffee shop to four times a week.		
Possible Amount to be Repurposed to Reduce or Pay Off Debts:		
Within 12 mos	Within 18 mos	Within 24 mos
$2736	$4104	$5472

Congratulations!!! Your child is graduating from daycare moving on to first grade in the public school district. For many parents, childcare costs approximately $800 a month. Once the child enters public school, this expense can be redirected to pay off or reduce another debt.		
Possible Amount to be Repurposed to Reduce or Pay Off Debts:		
Within 12 mos	Within 18 mos	Within 24 mos
$9600	$14,400	$19,200

2nd Level: Starting a Home-Based Business

Opportunity: Based on your skills and expertise, consider starting a service-based business that offers low startup costs, the potential to scale, and the ability to generate steady income without the need for inventory.

Starting a service-based business can be relatively easy and affordable, especially if it requires minimal upfront investment. Here are some service-based businesses that are easy to start and fund:

1. Freelancing Services

- Writing, graphic design, web development, and digital marketing.

  Requires only a laptop and internet connection; platforms like Upwork and Fiverr help find clients.

2. Consulting or Coaching
   - Business consulting, career coaching, fitness training, or life coaching.
     Minimal startup costs—just knowledge, expertise, and a website; can be done remotely via Zoom or Skype.
3. Cleaning Services
   - Residential or commercial cleaning requires basic supplies.
     Low overhead and easy to scale with more clients; can start solo and expand with employees.
4. Home or Virtual Assistance
   - Administrative support, bookkeeping, and social media management.
     Requires minimal equipment (computer, phone); clients range from small business owners to busy professionals.
5. Event Planning or Party Services
   - Wedding planning, corporate events, or kids' party planning.
     Low startup costs—mainly networking and organization skills; can partner with vendors for supplies instead of stocking inventory.
6. Pet Services
   - Dog walking, pet sitting, or grooming.
     Minimal equipment needed (leashes, treats, cleaning supplies); can be operated locally with little competition.
7. Tutoring or Teaching
   - Online or in-person tutoring in subjects like math, languages, or music.
     Uses existing knowledge—requires only marketing and materials; can charge hourly or package rates.

8. Delivery or Errand Services
    - Grocery shopping, package delivery, or personal shopping.
      Can use your own vehicle with minimal additional investment; apps like TaskRabbit or Instacart make it easy to find customers.
9. Landscaping or Handyman Services
    - Lawn care, painting, or minor repairs.
      Basic tools and skills needed; high demand in residential areas.
10. Fitness or Wellness Services
    - Personal training, yoga instruction, or massage therapy.
      Can start from home, parks, or online sessions; certification may be needed but costs are relatively low.

Each of these businesses can be started with minimal capital and scaled over time, based on demand and success.

3rd Level: Producing Multiple Streams of Residual Income

Opportunity: Use repurposed money from discretionary expenses or unnecessary items and revenue from the home-based business to generate multiple streams of residual income.

Residual income, also known as passive income, offers the significant benefit of generating ongoing earnings with minimal active effort once the initial work or investment is in place. This type of income provides financial stability and can supplement traditional earned income. Residual income streams can continue to flow, enabling families to explore new opportunities.

Here are several common sources of residual income:

1. Royalties from Intellectual Property

- Music Royalties: Musicians earn residual income when their songs are played on streaming services, radio, or licensed for commercials and movies.
- Book Royalties: Authors earn residual income from book sales and e-book downloads after publication.
- Patent Royalties: Inventors can license their patents and earn residual income as companies use their inventions.

2. Online Course Sales

- Example: If you create and sell an online course on platforms like Udemy or Teachable, you can continue to earn money each time someone purchases or enrolls in the course, even after the initial creation.

3. Affiliate Marketing

- Example: By promoting products or services online and earning a commission for each sale generated through your affiliate link, you can earn passive income from successful referrals, even after the initial promotion.

4. Peer-to-Peer Lending

- Example: By lending money to individuals or small businesses through platforms like Lending Club or Prosper, you earn residual income in the form of interest payments as the loans are repaid.

5. Subscription-Based Businesses

- Example: Offering a subscription service (e.g., software, newsletters, membership sites) generates recurring monthly or yearly income from subscribers, which can be residual once the service is established.

6. YouTube or Podcast Ad Revenue

    - Example: Content creators on platforms like YouTube or podcasts can generate ongoing residual income through ads or sponsorships. Once content is created, views or listens can continue generating revenue over time.

7. Licensing of Digital Assets

    - Example: Selling digital products like stock photos, videos, or design templates through platforms like Shutterstock or Adobe Stock can generate residual income each time your assets are downloaded.

8. App or Software Sales

    - Example: If you develop an app or software and list it on app stores or sell licenses, you can earn residual income from sales and in-app purchases long after the development phase is complete.

9. Peer-to-Peer Car Rentals

    - Example: Services like Turo allow you to rent out your car when you're not using it, generating residual income from the rental fees.

10. Network Marketing

    - Example: Many multi-level marketing (MLM) companies offer residual income opportunities where you earn commissions not only on your sales but also on sales made by those in your downline.

Residual income sources are valuable for creating financial freedom and security, as they provide ongoing income with minimal ongoing effort.

Residual income refers to earnings that continue to flow after the initial work is completed or investment has been made. It comes from various sources, such as royalties from intellectual property or business systems that operate independently of the business owner's direct involvement.

One of the primary benefits of residual income is financial freedom, as it allows individuals to earn money without continuous effort, providing stability and potentially supplementing or even replacing active income. This type of income also offers flexibility, allowing people to focus on other projects, enjoy more leisure time, or reinvest in new opportunities for wealth generation.

4th Level: <u>Generating Income-Producing Assets</u>

<u>Opportunity</u>: Using the revenue earned from multiple income streams (Level 3) will allow you to invest in assets that create cash flow, aka income-producing assets.

An asset is anything of value that an individual, business, or organization owns, which can be used to generate income, provide future benefits, or cover liabilities. Income-producing assets are investments that generate regular earnings, such as interest, dividends, or rental income, without the need for constant active involvement. Examples include real estate properties, dividend-paying stocks, bonds, intellectual property, and businesses. These assets help individuals build wealth by providing a steady cash flow and, in many cases, appreciating in value over time.

Here are a few income-producing assets to generate regular cash flow:

1 of 5 – <u>Rental Properties</u> (Income-Producing Asset)

Rental properties are one of the most popular income-producing assets, offering investors the ability to generate steady cash flow through monthly rent payments. When an investor purchases a residential or commercial property and leases it to tenants, the rental income can cover the property's expenses and provide additional profit. Rental properties are attractive because they offer both immediate income and the potential for long-term capital appreciation as the property value increases over time.

The primary way rental properties produce income is through rent payments from tenants. After covering costs such as mortgage payments, property taxes, insurance, maintenance, and property management fees, the remaining rental income becomes profit. The key to successful income generation from rental properties is finding tenants who can reliably pay rent and setting rent prices that balance being competitive in the market with covering the costs and generating positive cash flow. In many cases, rental property investors benefit from increasing rents over time, as the market allows, further boosting their income stream.

Another advantage of rental properties as an income-producing asset is their potential for appreciation. Over the long term, property values tend to increase, allowing the investor to build equity. As the mortgage is paid down and the property appreciates, the investor's ownership stake in the property grows. This combination of cash flow and equity growth makes rental properties a powerful tool for wealth accumulation. Furthermore, rental property owners may also take advantage of tax benefits, such as deducting expenses like mortgage interest, repairs, and depreciation, which can reduce taxable income and enhance profitability.

In addition to providing monthly income, rental properties also offer flexibility in terms of diversification and investment strategy. Investors can choose between different types of rental properties, such as single-family homes, multifamily units, vacation rentals, or commercial properties, depending on their risk tolerance and financial goals. They can also diversify geographically by investing in different real estate markets, spreading their risk and potentially increasing returns. Some investors even explore short-term rental markets, such as Airbnb, to maximize their income potential, though this often requires more active management.

2 of 5 –Mutual Funds (Income-Producing Asset)

Mutual funds pool investors' money into a diversified portfolio of stocks, bonds, or other assets managed by professionals, providing convenience but often with higher fees and no guaranteed returns. Mutual funds are widely regarded as income-producing assets due to their ability to generate regular income for investors through various distributions, including dividends and interest. A mutual fund pools money from multiple investors to invest in a diversified portfolio of stocks, bonds, or other securities. This pooling of resources allows investors to access a wide range of asset classes, which can provide a steady stream of income while spreading risk. Income-focused mutual funds, such as those that invest in dividend-paying stocks or bonds, are particularly popular among investors seeking reliable cash flow.

One of the primary ways mutual funds generate income is through dividend payments from the stocks held in their portfolios. When a mutual fund invests in companies that pay dividends, it collects these payments and, after deducting expenses, distributes the income to its shareholders. Similarly, mutual funds that invest in bonds earn interest payments, which can also be distributed to investors. Many mutual funds offer automatic reinvestment options, allowing investors to reinvest their income distributions to purchase more shares, which can enhance long-term growth through compounding.

In addition to providing regular income, mutual funds also offer investors a level of professional management and diversification that may be difficult to achieve through individual investments. Fund managers utilize their expertise to select securities that align with the fund's investment objectives, actively managing the portfolio to maximize income potential while minimizing risks. This professional oversight can be particularly beneficial for investors who may lack the time or expertise to manage their investments actively. By investing in a mutual fund, investors can benefit from a well-researched and diversified approach to generating income, making mutual funds an appealing option for those looking to create a balanced income-generating portfolio.

3 of 5– Bonds (Income-Producing Asset)

Bonds are a classic type of income-producing asset that provides investors with a source of regular income and predictable cash flow through interest payments, often called coupon payments. When an investor purchases a bond, they are essentially lending money to the bond issuer—whether it's a government, municipality, or corporation—in exchange for periodic interest payments and the return of the bond's face value when it matures. These interest payments are fixed and typically paid semi-annually, making bonds particularly appealing for investors who seek a reliable income stream with relatively lower risk compared to stocks.

Governments, municipal entities, and corporations issue bonds as a way to raise capital. Bonds are similar to loans made by investors to the bond issuer. When an investor buys a bond, they are essentially lending money to the issuing entity—whether it's a government, corporation, or municipality. In return, the issuer agrees to pay the investor periodic interest (the coupon) and repay the principal amount (the face value of the bond) at a set maturity date.

Bonds can be issued by various types of public and private organizations to raise capital for different purposes:

- For governments, bonds help fund public projects like infrastructure development, education, or defense without immediately raising taxes.
- Municipal entities, such as cities, counties, or states, issue bonds to raise funds for public projects and infrastructure improvements. These projects might include building schools, roads, hospitals, water systems, or other essential services that benefit the community.

- Corporations issue bonds to finance expansions, new projects, or to restructure existing debt. By issuing bonds, governments, municipal entities, and corporations borrow money from investors, agreeing to pay back the principal amount on a specific date, along with periodic interest payments. This allows them to secure large amounts of funding while spreading the cost of repayment over time.

In summary, bonds are an effective income-producing asset due to their fixed interest payments, capital preservation, and relative stability. They provide a consistent income stream, making them particularly suitable for income-seeking investors who prefer lower-risk investments. Whether through government, corporate, or municipal bonds, these securities play a crucial role in balancing portfolios and providing dependable returns.

4 of 5 – <u>Real Estate Investment Trust "REITs"</u> (Income-Producing Assets)

REITs are an excellent example of an income-producing asset, offering investors regular dividend payments derived from income-generating real estate. REITs are companies that own, manage, or finance various types of real estate, such as office buildings, apartments, shopping centers, and hotels. The primary way REITs produce income is through the rent collected from tenants occupying the properties they own. These rental payments generate steady and predictable revenue, which is passed on to shareholders in the form of dividend payments. They are required by law to distribute a significant portion of their earnings to shareholders in the form of dividends, making them a reliable source of consistent cash flow.

Investing in REITs allows you to earn a share of the income generated by commercial real estate without owning physical property. Dividends paid by REITs provide residual income. For income-seeking investors, particularly those looking for passive income, REITs provide a unique opportunity to benefit from the real estate market without directly owning physical property.

In many cases, REITs offer higher dividend yields compared to other dividend-paying stocks, as they are structured to focus on income distribution. Higher-dividend yields in connection with Real Estate Investment Trusts (REITs) refer to the percentage of a REIT's annual dividend payments relative to its share price. REITs are required by law to distribute at least 90% of their taxable income to shareholders in the form of dividends. This makes REITs particularly attractive for investors seeking regular income streams.

In addition to their consistent dividend payments, REITs also offer the potential for capital appreciation as the value of their underlying real estate assets increases over time. As real estate properties appreciate, the overall value of the REIT rises, which can lead to higher stock prices and larger dividend payouts. REITs also have the ability to grow their portfolios by acquiring new properties or developing existing ones, further boosting their income-generating potential. This combination of income and growth makes REITs a compelling option for investors who want both regular cash flow and long-term wealth accumulation.

Moreover, REITs provide a way to diversify within the real estate sector without the burden of directly managing properties. Investors can choose from different types of REITs, such as equity REITs, which own and operate properties, or mortgage REITs, which provide financing for real estate and earn income from interest on mortgage loans. There are also specialized REITs focused on sectors like healthcare, data centers, and infrastructure, offering even greater diversification. This variety allows investors to access different segments of the real estate market with less risk than owning individual properties while still earning regular income.

In summary, REITs are a powerful income-producing asset because of their high dividend yields, consistent payments, and potential for growing distributions over time. They are considered an attractive income stream for investors seeking a balance of income stability and growth potential. REITs play an essential role in a well-rounded investment portfolio.

5 of 5 – Exchange-Traded Funds "ETFs" (Income-Producing Asset)

ETFs are investment funds that are traded on stock exchanges, similar to individual stocks. ETFs provide diversification by pooling a wide range of assets, such as stocks, bonds, or commodities, into a single investment, which helps spread risk and reduces the impact of poor performance from individual securities.

Exchange-Traded Funds (ETFs) are increasingly recognized as effective income-producing assets, offering investors regular cash flow through dividends and interest payments. Similar to mutual funds, ETFs pool money from multiple investors to invest in a diversified portfolio of securities, which can include dividend-paying stocks, bonds, or other income-generating assets. As the underlying securities generate income, ETFs distribute these earnings to shareholders in the form of dividends, typically on a quarterly basis.

One of the key advantages of ETFs as income-producing assets is their liquidity, allowing investors to buy and sell shares throughout the trading day at market prices, much like individual stocks. This flexibility enables investors to quickly respond to market conditions while still benefiting from a diversified investment strategy.

In summary: With their combination of diversification, liquidity, and potential for consistent income, ETFs serve as a compelling choice for investors seeking to build a steady stream of cash flow while participating in broader market trends.

$ $

Investing in securities through a brokerage firm involves several key steps. First, you need to open a brokerage account by selecting a reputable brokerage firm and completing an application with personal and financial information. Next, fund your account by transferring money from your bank account or another investment account. Once funded, you can research and select securities based on your investment goals, whether stocks, bonds, mutual funds, or ETFs. After selecting an asset, you place an order through the brokerage platform, choosing between market, limit, or stop orders depending on your strategy. Finally, you should monitor and manage your investments, regularly reviewing performance and making adjustments as needed to align with your financial objectives.

Disclaimer from the author: The information provided herein is for educational and informational purposes only and should not be construed as financial, investment, or legal advice. Investing in securities, including stocks, mutual funds, ETFs, REITs, and bonds, carries inherent risks, including the potential loss of principal. Before making any investment decisions, readers and investors should conduct their own research, assess their risk tolerance, and consult with a qualified financial advisor or professional.

Next Level Abundance IS POSSIBLE

Two years ago, David and his family began their journey to next level abundance, generating income from one level to the next with the intention of the using multiple income streams to fund each income-producing asset as illustrated below:

- David earns residual income teaching an online course. He teaches other families how to start and maintain investment accounts on behalf of the families' children. The course is sold repeatedly to an unlimited number of students without the need for additional resources, allowing for continuous earnings with minimal ongoing effort. The online courses reach a global audience, providing access to a larger market, and making online course sales a lucrative source of income for David. The income David earns from the online course allows him to invest in EFTs as an income-producing asset, offering regular cash flow through dividends and interest payments.

- Cathy, David's sister, partnered with her husband to earn residual income via Peer-to-Peer Lending. Becoming a peer-to-peer (P2P) lender typically starts by selecting a reputable P2P lending platform, such as Prosper or Lending Club. Once an account is created, the lender deposits funds, which will be used to issue loans to borrowers on the platform. After funding loans, the lender receives regular payments that include both principal and interest, which can be reinvested or withdrawn. P2P platforms handle the loan servicing, making it relatively hands-off for the lender once the initial investments are made. With the income Cathy and her husband earn as P2P lenders, they have chosen to invest in bonds as an income-producing asset. The return of principal, combined with the interest income, can make bonds a low-risk option for investors looking to safeguard their capital while still earning income.
- James, David's brother receives residual income via his YouTube channel and Affiliate Marketing. A person can earn lucrative income on YouTube through multiple revenue streams, the most common being ad revenue generated from views on their videos. As their channel grows and attracts more subscribers and views, YouTube pays them a percentage of ad revenue through the YouTube Partner Program. Additionally, creators can generate income through sponsorships, where brands pay them to promote products, as well as through affiliate marketing, selling merchandise, and fan support via memberships or platforms like Patreon. With consistent content and a dedicated audience, as a YouTube creator, James has turned his YouTube channel into a profitable business. To generate income-producing assets, James has chosen to invest in REITs because they provide a way for him to

earn passive income without the complexities of owning and managing physical properties.

- Sherri and Mark, David's parents, own and operate a daycare center as their primary business. They earn multiple streams of income subletting the day care building as an event space to other small business owners, merchants, and vendors. The couple earns additional income renting the building for weddings, baby showers, and birthday parties; community events, meetings, workshops and seminars; as well as Sunday church services for a local congregation.

  The revenue earned from all these income streams allows Sherri and Mark to expand their business by opening another day care center in a nearby community. This new day care center will offer more comprehensive services designed specifically for single moms with school-age children: i.e., before and after school childcare; shuttle bus to transport children to and from school; weekend childcare for parents who work weekend shifts; childcare for summer, spring and winter breaks as well as childcare when school is closed to observe a holiday but parents are assigned to work. Operating an additional day care business is a lucrative income-producing asset for Sherri and Mark.
- Nicole, David's cousin, earns rental income from two different rental properties. Originally, she purchased a four-unit multifamily apartment. A few years later, she purchased her second property, a 12-unit apartment building, as additional rental income.

  To expand her real estate portfolio, Nicole has decided to purchase a 24-unit multifamily property.

  To fund the downpayment, she will use the cash value in her dividend-paying whole life insurance policy. She decides to borrow against the cash value of the insurance policy to fund the downpayment. Ten years ago, Nicole purchased a dividend-paying whole life insurance policy.

A whole life insurance policy is a type of permanent life insurance that provides coverage for the policyholder's entire lifetime as long as premiums are paid. Premiums are typically fixed and do not increase with age. The annual premium in a whole life insurance policy is the fixed amount the policyholder pays each year to keep the policy active.

The death benefit in a whole life insurance policy is the lump-sum payment that the insurance company provides to the beneficiary upon the policyholder's death. It is typically tax-free and ensures financial protection for the beneficiary, helping cover expenses such as funeral costs, debts, and income replacement. In addition to the guaranteed death benefit for beneficiaries, the policy has a cash value component that grows over time.

The cash value of a whole life insurance policy is a tax-deferred savings component that grows over time. The policyholder can borrow against or withdraw from the cash value. Borrowing against the cash value of a whole-life insurance policy involves taking a loan from the insurance company using the accumulated cash value as collateral. The policyholder can request a loan up to a certain percentage of the cash value. Typically, a policyholder can borrow 70% to 90% of the cash value of a whole-life insurance policy. The exact percentage depends on the specific terms of the policy.

Purchasing Paid-Up Additions (PUAs) helps build up the cash value of a whole life insurance policy. A Paid-Up Additions (PUA) Rider is an optional feature in a Whole Life Insurance policy that allows policyholders to purchase additional fully paid-up life insurance coverage using dividends or extra premium payments. These paid-up additions increase the policy's death benefit and cash value over time.

Within a dividend-paying whole life insurance policy, the PUAs generate their own dividends that compound over time, further boosting the cash value. This strategy enhances the policy's overall value and can increase the amount available for loans or withdrawals.

Borrowing against the cash value of a whole-life insurance policy offers several benefits. It provides quick access to funds without a credit check or lengthy approval process, making it a convenient option for emergencies or large expenses. Interest is charged on the loan, and if it's not repaid, the outstanding balance, including interest, is deducted from the death benefit. Unlike traditional loans, the unpaid interest can compound, reducing the policy's value over time.

The loan is flexible, with no fixed repayment schedule, allowing the policyholder to repay at their own pace. Additionally, interest rates are often lower than traditional personal loans or credit cards. As long as the loan is repaid, the policy's death benefit remains intact, making it a useful financial tool while still maintaining life insurance coverage.

Using her dividend-paying whole life insurance to generate additional income-producing assets was a smart money decision for Nicole. Let me explain why.

Applying the cash value of a whole life insurance policy to fund real estate deals offers several advantages. First, it provides liquidity, allowing Nicole to access funds without relying on traditional bank loans or credit approvals. Second, she can take out a tax-free loan against the cash value, preserving the insurance policy's growth while using the funds for real estate purchases, renovations, or down payments. Additionally, since the cash value continues to grow even while borrowed against, Nicole can benefit from compound interest and policy dividends. This strategy also offers asset protection, as life insurance loans are typically not reported to credit bureaus, reducing financial risk.

A whole life insurance policy is a powerful way to invest in real estate. Owning rental property as an income-producing asset offers several key benefits: immediate cash flow through rental payments while generating multiple streams of income.

Summary: By starting where you are [at your current financial level], using what you have [opportunities, information, resources], and doing what you can [taking action, following through, being consistent], adult family members are given the opportunity to prosper by advancing from one financial level to the next.

CONCLUSION: CHAPTER 5 (OPPORTUNITY TO PROSPER)

Arriving at your destination

Arriving at Level 4, owning income-producing assets means having your financial needs and goals consistently met without stress or strain. Bills are paid on time, debt is managed or eliminated, and there's no worrying about meeting basic needs such as housing, food, or heath care, as owning income-producing assets provides a comfortable level of financial freedom.

At this point, investments are growing steadily, and there's a comfortable cushion of savings for both short-term needs and unexpected emergencies. Financial decisions are made with confidence rather than fear. You're experiencing the peace of mind that comes from knowing that your finances are under control and working for you, not the other way around.

At this level, you are able to enjoy life's pleasures, whether it's traveling, pursuing hobbies, or giving back to others through charitable organizations, philanthropy, or community development projects.

Perhaps the most defining aspect of an abundant lifestyle is the ability to choose how to spend your time. Financial freedom is living life on your own terms, doing what brings fulfillment, and spending quality time with loved ones. Owning your time is one of the most valuable assets to be achieved.

The main focus going forward is on long-term growth rather than short-term survival. You're now in a position to build generational wealth to establish a strong family legacy.

Attributes of a Strong Family Legacy

A strong family legacy built on generational wealth goes beyond financial assets; it includes values, education, and a shared vision for the future. Financial literacy is a key component, ensuring that future generations understand how to manage, grow, and preserve wealth. Strong family values—such as unity, discipline, loyalty, integrity, mutual respect, and generosity—help guide responsible decision-making and encourage the next generation to uphold and build upon the family's legacy.

Estate planning, including trusts and wills, ensures that wealth is passed down efficiently while minimizing potential conflicts. Investing in education, mentorship, and business opportunities for younger generations strengthens their ability to sustain and expand the family's wealth. Ultimately, a lasting legacy is built on a foundation of financial wisdom, strong relationships, and a commitment to stewardship.

It's important to encourage the next generation to be open to learning by teaching financial literacy, reinforcing good financial habits to make smart money decisions, collaborating, sharing knowledge, and learning from mistakes.

A family legacy is built upon a foundation in much the same way that a structure relies on a solid base for stability and strength. This foundation in a family consists of core values, principles, and bonds that guide the relationships and interactions among its family members. Trust, discipline, communication, and mutual respect are key elements of this foundation, providing the support needed for the family to thrive.

$ $

CHAPTER 6: OPPORTUNITY TO THRIVE

Creating a family trust is a strategic way to preserve and transfer generational wealth while ensuring that the family continues to thrive for future generations. A well-structured trust protects assets from unnecessary taxes, legal disputes, and mismanagement, allowing wealth to grow and benefit multiple heirs. It also provides a framework for passing down family values and financial principles, ensuring that wealth is used responsibly. By establishing clear guidelines and appointing a trusted fiduciary, a family can create a lasting legacy that supports education, business ventures, and philanthropic efforts for generations to come.

Establishing a family trust enables a family to thrive by providing a structured and secure way to protect and preserve family wealth. A family trust is a legal arrangement in which a trustee holds and manages various assets for the benefit of specific family members, known as beneficiaries. The primary purpose of a family trust is to ensure efficient management of assets and to make the transfer of wealth easier from generation to generation.

A trustee is the individuals or entities managing the trust. Beneficiaries are those who will benefit from the trust. Assets are resources owned or controlled by an individual, business, or entity that have economic value and can provide future benefits.

<u>Primary advantages of a family trust</u>

A family trust is designed to protect and preserve wealth, often with the intent of passing it down through generations while minimizing taxes, legal challenges, and probate costs. One of the primary advantages of a family trust is its ability to protect assets from external risks, such as lawsuits, creditors, or even the mismanagement of wealth by heirs. Since the assets in a family trust are legally owned by the trust and not by the individual beneficiaries, they are generally shielded from personal liabilities or legal claims. This protection ensures that family wealth remains intact and can be passed down to future generations without being diminished by unforeseen financial or legal issues.

Duties of the Trustee

A trustee's duties include managing and safeguarding the trust's assets, making distributions to beneficiaries according to the trust's terms, and acting in the best interest of the beneficiaries with loyalty, impartiality, and prudence.

Before the family appoints a trustee for the family trust, several candidates can be considered, each offering distinct advantages. Professional trustees, such as lawyers, accountants, or corporate fiduciaries, provide expertise and objectivity, ensuring compliance with legal and financial regulations, but they typically charge fees for their services. In some cases, co-trustees are appointed, combining the personal insight of a family member with the professional knowledge of a corporate or professional trustee, creating a balanced approach.

Trustees must ensure that they follow the trust agreement, which outlines how the trust's assets are to be managed, distributed, and protected.

Trustees are responsible for managing and maintaining a family trust according to the terms set out in the trust document. Here's how and where trustees typically maintain a family trust:

1. Trust Documents and Legal Compliance

- **How**: Trustees must ensure that they follow the trust agreement, which outlines how the trust's assets are to be managed, distributed, and protected. They must act in the best interests of the beneficiaries and adhere to fiduciary duties such as loyalty, care, and impartiality.

- **Where**: The original trust documents are usually stored in a safe location such as a lawyer's office, a bank's safe deposit box, or securely at the trustee's home. Copies may be kept by the trustee, beneficiaries, or a trusted advisor.

2. Opening a Trust Bank Account

- **How**: Trustees typically open a dedicated bank account in the name of the trust to hold liquid assets such as cash or income-producing investments. This ensures transparency and proper tracking of trust transactions, such as incoming dividends, interest, or payments to beneficiaries.
- **Where**: A trust bank account is opened at a financial institution. The trustee must provide the trust document and tax identification number (TIN) to the bank.

3. Managing and Investing Trust Assets

- **How**: Trustees are responsible for managing the assets held in the trust, which may include real estate, stocks, bonds, businesses, or other valuables. They must invest trust assets prudently, often in accordance with the "Prudent Investor Rule," which mandates a balance between risk and return.
- **Where**: Investment accounts for the trust may be opened with brokerage firms or financial institutions. If the trust holds real estate or other tangible property, the trustee must ensure proper maintenance, insurance, and management of those assets.

4. Record Keeping and Accounting

- **How**: Trustees are required to maintain detailed records of all trust transactions, including income, expenses, distributions, and investments. Regular accounting must be provided to beneficiaries, showing how the assets are managed and distributed.

- **Where**: Records are often kept digitally (using accounting software) or in physical files at the trustee's office or with their financial advisor or accountant. Proper documentation is critical in case of disputes or audits.

5. Tax Filing and Compliance

- **How**: Trustees are responsible for filing annual tax returns on behalf of the trust (if applicable), reporting income, and paying any required taxes. Trusts often have their own tax identification number, and trustees must ensure compliance with federal and state tax laws.
- **Where**: Tax filings are submitted to tax authorities (IRS in the U.S. or relevant tax agencies elsewhere). The trustee may work with a tax advisor or accountant to ensure proper filing and compliance.

6. Distributing Trust Assets to Beneficiaries

- **How**: Trustees must follow the terms of the trust when distributing assets to beneficiaries, whether through regular payments, one-time lump sums, or conditional distributions based on milestones (e.g., reaching a certain age).
- **Where**: The trust must distribute all of its income to the beneficiaries each year. This includes interest, dividends, and rental income. Distributions can be made from the trust's bank or investment accounts directly to beneficiaries' accounts or through other methods such as checks, electronic transfers, or direct asset transfers.

7. Safeguarding Physical Assets

- **How**: Trustees may need to protect and maintain physical assets like real estate, artwork, or collectibles held in the trust. This includes ensuring the assets are insured and maintained properly.
- **Where**: Physical assets might be stored in specialized facilities, such as vaults for precious items or professionally managed properties for real estate holdings.

8. Working with Advisors

- **How**: Trustees often collaborate with financial advisors, attorneys, tax professionals, and estate planners to ensure the trust is managed properly and aligned with the grantor's wishes.
- **Where**: Meetings with advisors take place in financial institutions, law offices, or remotely using online tools.

By following these steps and working in a diligent, transparent manner, trustees ensure the family trust is properly managed, complies with legal requirements, and best serves the beneficiaries.

Trust Deed

The **family trust deed** plays a crucial role in preparing the **family trust agreement** as it serves as the foundational document that outlines the specific terms and conditions of the trust. Here's how the family trust deed factors into the preparation of the family trust agreement:

1. Establishing the Trust's Purpose

The trust deed specifies the purpose of the trust, such as asset protection, estate planning, or providing for beneficiaries' education. This purpose must be reflected in the trust agreement to ensure that all provisions align with the intended goals of the trust.

2. Defining Key Parties

The trust deed identifies the grantor (the person creating the trust), the trustee(s) (the individuals or entities managing the trust), and the beneficiaries (those who will benefit from the trust). These roles and their responsibilities are crucial components of the trust agreement and must be clearly stated for legal clarity and compliance.

3. Outlining Trust Terms and Conditions

The trust deed details the specific rules governing the management and distribution of trust assets, including how income and principal are to be allocated to beneficiaries. The trust agreement must incorporate these terms to ensure that the trustee has clear guidelines to follow and that beneficiaries understand their rights.

4. Incorporating Asset Management Guidelines

The trust deed may specify how the trust assets are to be invested and managed, including any restrictions or guidelines for the trustee. These investment strategies and management guidelines need to be documented in the trust agreement to provide a roadmap for the trustee's actions.

5. Addressing Successor Trustees

The trust deed often includes provisions for appointing successor trustees in case the original trustee is unable to fulfill their duties. This information is vital for the trust agreement to ensure smooth transitions in management and continuity of the trust's operations.

6. Specifying Distribution Terms

The trust deed outlines the conditions under which beneficiaries will receive distributions from the trust, such as reaching a certain age or fulfilling specific conditions. These conditions must be clearly articulated in the trust agreement to ensure that all parties understand the distribution process and timelines.

7. Ensuring Legal Compliance

The trust deed must comply with relevant laws and regulations to be valid and enforceable. The trust agreement should be crafted with legal considerations in mind, reflecting the provisions of the trust deed and adhering to applicable laws governing trusts.

8. Incorporating Amendment Procedures

The trust deed may contain clauses detailing how the trust can be amended or revoked. It's important to include these amendment procedures in the trust agreement to ensure that changes can be made legally and in accordance with the grantor's wishes.

In summary, the **family trust deed** serves as the legal foundation that guides the preparation of the **family trust agreement**. The trust agreement must reflect the terms outlined in the deed, ensuring clarity, compliance, and a clear understanding of the roles and responsibilities of all parties involved.

Components of the Family Trust Agreement

A **family trust agreement** is a legal document that outlines the structure and management of assets placed in trust for the benefit of family members. It outlines how the trust will be managed and distributed. Below is a simplified example of a family trust agreement.

The terms within a family trust define how the trust operates and outlines specific instructions for managing and distributing assets. These terms typically include details about who the beneficiaries are, who the trustee is (the person or entity responsible for managing the trust), and what powers and responsibilities the trustee holds. The trust may also specify the conditions under which assets are to be distributed, such as age milestones, educational achievements, or other life events. Additionally, the terms can outline investment strategies, specify how income generated by the trust should be handled, and provide guidance on how to handle special circumstances, such as medical needs or financial emergencies. These carefully crafted terms ensure that the family's wealth is managed according to their wishes while also providing flexibility to adapt to changing circumstances over time.

Key components of the family trust agreement include the grantor's name (the individual establishing the trust), the trustee's name and address (individuals or institutions responsible for managing the trust), and the beneficiaries' names (the family members who will benefit from the trust). The agreement details the trust's purpose, which may range from providing financial security to funding education or preserving wealth for future generations. It also specifies the assets to be included in the trust, such as cash, real estate, or investments, and defines the terms and conditions for managing and distributing those assets, including any restrictions or specific milestones (e.g., beneficiaries reaching a certain age). Additionally, it outlines the trustee's responsibilities and powers, including provisions for investment decisions and tax compliance, as well as any instructions regarding the duration of the trust or its termination. The agreement may also include guidelines for successor trustees, conflict resolution, and other essential governance measures.

DISCLAIMER: It's important to consult with a lawyer when drafting an actual trust agreement, as laws vary by jurisdiction, and specifics will need to be tailored to individual circumstances.

Assets typically included in a family trust

Real estate is often a primary asset, encompassing family homes, vacation properties, and investment properties. Financial assets, such as stocks, bonds, mutual funds, and cash accounts, are also commonly included to ensure long-term growth and liquidity. Business interests, like shares in a family-owned company, can be placed in the trust to ensure continued family control. Life insurance policies may be added to provide financial security for beneficiaries. Additionally, valuable personal items such as jewelry, artwork, and collectibles can be part of the trust to safeguard high-value possessions. By including these diverse assets, a family trust offers a comprehensive way to protect and manage wealth for future generations.

Distribution of assets

The trust outlines specific terms for how and when assets are distributed, ensuring that the family's wealth remains intact for future generations. Trust deeds can be drafted to include provisions that dictate when and how assets are distributed, such as for education, housing, or business ventures. This control helps prevent heirs from squandering the family's wealth or making poor financial decisions. Additionally, because the trustee oversees the management of the trust, the assets can be professionally managed and invested, helping to grow the family's wealth over time. By ensuring that wealth is not only preserved but also responsibly distributed and invested, a family trust can support multiple generations, creating long-term financial stability.

Opportunity to Protect and Preserve the Family's Assets

A family trust is a powerful legal tool that helps protect and preserve a family's assets for future generations. By placing assets such as property, investments, and business interests in a trust, a family can ensure those assets are managed and distributed according to their wishes, while also shielding them from potential risks like creditors, lawsuits, and estate taxes. Below are several scenarios that illustrate how a family trust can safeguard assets and provide financial security:

Scenario 1: Protection from Creditors

Imagine a family that owns a lucrative real estate portfolio consisting of rental properties and commercial buildings. One of the family members operates a business that, while successful, carries some risk of financial liability. Without a family trust, the family's personal assets, including the real estate portfolio, could be exposed to creditors if the business fails or if a lawsuit arises. By placing the assets in a family trust, the real estate holdings are separated from the individual family member's personal liabilities. This means that even if a lawsuit is filed against the business or the family member, creditors would have no claim to the trust's assets, ensuring that the family's wealth is protected.

Scenario 2: Preserving Wealth for Future Generations

In another scenario, a couple with substantial financial investments and properties wishes to leave an inheritance to their children and grandchildren. However, they are concerned that their children may not manage the assets responsibly or that the money could be wasted. A family trust allows the couple to set specific conditions for how the assets will be used. For example, the trust could dictate that the children receive distributions only for specific purposes, such as education, buying a home, or starting a business. The trust can also ensure that the wealth is passed down through generations, avoiding premature depletion. Additionally, the assets remain protected from external threats such as the children's creditors or potential divorce settlements, preserving the family's wealth for the long term.

Scenario 3: Avoiding Probate and Reducing Estate Taxes

When a person dies, their estate typically goes through a legal process known as probate, where the assets are distributed according to their will or state law. Probate can be time-consuming, costly, and public, which may expose the estate to legal challenges or unwanted attention. By establishing a family trust, the assets held within the trust bypass probate entirely, allowing for a smooth and private transfer of wealth to the beneficiaries. Furthermore, a well-structured trust can reduce or even eliminate estate taxes, ensuring that a larger portion of the family's wealth is preserved for future generations. This can be particularly beneficial for families with high-value estates, as it mitigates the financial burden of estate taxes that would otherwise reduce the inheritance.

Scenario 4: Protecting Assets During Illness or Disability

Another critical aspect of a family trust is its ability to safeguard assets in the event of a family member's illness or disability. Consider a situation where one parent is diagnosed with a degenerative illness that requires long-term care. Without a trust, the family might have to sell off significant assets or deplete their savings to cover medical expenses and care. A family trust, however, can be structured to ensure that assets are protected while still allowing for the parent's medical needs to be met. The trust can appoint a trustee to manage the assets and make financial decisions in the best interest of the family member, avoiding the need for a court-appointed guardian or conservatorship.

In all of these scenarios, a family trust serves as a valuable tool for asset protection, allowing the family to maintain control over their wealth while shielding it from external risks and ensuring it is distributed according to their wishes.

Summary:

Thriving financially involves more than just accumulating wealth; it requires thoughtful planning, disciplined management, and a long-term vision. It begins with building a strong foundation, such as creating a budget, saving consistently, and investing strategically to grow assets over time. Diversifying income streams, managing debt effectively, and leveraging tax-advantaged accounts or tools like trusts also play a crucial role in securing financial stability. Beyond wealth accumulation, thriving financially means maintaining financial independence, preparing for unexpected challenges, and passing on a solid financial legacy to future generations. It empowers individuals and families to achieve their goals, pursue opportunities, and enjoy greater peace of mind.

<u>Scenarios of various asset distribution and trust term options</u>

Scenario #1

A family trust is set up by a couple (David and his wife Regina) for their two children. The trust terms specify that upon the death of both parents, the trust's assets will be split equally between the children. However, each child will only gain full access to their share when they turn 30.

- **Explanation:** This scenario allows the assets to be distributed in a way that gives children time to mature before receiving significant financial resources, reducing the risk of irresponsible spending.
- **Trust Term:** Distribution of Assets upon Death

Scenario #2

The trust agreement between Mike and his wife Cathy, as well as David and his wife Regina, specifies that after (the "grantor") passes away, the surviving spouse will receive all income generated by the trust's investments. The principal (the original assets placed in the trust) will not be distributed until after the death of the surviving spouse.

- **Explanation:** This ensures that the surviving spouse is financially supported for the rest of their life, while the assets are preserved for future beneficiaries (e.g., children or grandchildren) upon the spouse's death.
- **Trust Term:** Income for Surviving Spouse

Scenario #3

All of the adults in the family with young children (David, Nicole, Cathy, and James) create a trust that designates a specific amount to each of their children for educational purposes.

- **Explanation:** Specifying trust terms for educational purposes ensures that funds are used exclusively for the beneficiaries' academic needs, helping them achieve long-term educational goals.
- **Trust Term:** Education Funds for Beneficiaries

Scenario #4

Nicole, David's cousin, created a family trust stating that her son, nieces, and nephews as beneficiaries will each receive distributions based on achieving certain milestones. For example, the trust will distribute $50,000 to each beneficiary upon obtaining a college degree, $100,000 for purchasing a first home, and an additional $200,000 when the beneficiary reaches the age of 40.

- **Explanation:** This scenario encourages beneficiaries to meet certain personal and professional goals before receiving distributions. It can be used to promote responsible behavior, education, and financial planning.
- **Trust Term:** Incentive Trust for Career Milestones

Scenario #5

David and Regina have two children who are both beneficiaries. One of the beneficiaries has a disability. The trust includes a special needs trust provision that ensures the disabled beneficiary receives distributions in a way that does not disqualify them from government benefits, such as Supplemental Security Income (SSI) or Medicaid. The trustee is instructed to use funds for the beneficiary's medical, educational, and recreational needs without direct payments that would affect eligibility for public assistance.

- **Explanation:** This type of provision protects a beneficiary with special needs, ensuring they continue to receive necessary government benefits while still benefiting from the trust.
- **Trust Term: Special Needs Trust Provision**

Scenario #6

The trust agreement gives the trustee discretion to make distributions based on the financial needs of the beneficiaries. For example, if a beneficiary encounters medical emergencies, the trustee can distribute funds to cover those costs. There is no fixed schedule for distributions; instead, the trustee decides based on specific criteria such as need, health, and financial stability.

- **Explanation:** This type of term provides flexibility, allowing the trustee to respond to beneficiaries' individual circumstances over time. It can be especially useful if the grantor wants the trust to adapt to unforeseen events.
- **Trust Term: Discretionary Distributions**

Scenario #7

The trust includes a spendthrift clause, which prevents the beneficiaries from selling, pledging, or otherwise transferring their interest in the trust to creditors or third parties. The trustee has sole discretion to distribute funds to the beneficiaries directly for their living expenses or other needs.

- **Explanation:** A spendthrift clause protects the trust assets from being squandered by the beneficiaries or claimed by creditors, ensuring the assets are used for their intended purposes.
- **Trust Term:** Spendthrift Clause

Scenario #8

Sherri and Mark, David's parents, have substantial financial investments and properties. They wish to leave an inheritance to their children and grandchildren. A family trust allows the couple to set specific conditions for how the assets will be used. For example, the trust dictates that the children and grandchildren receive distributions only for specific purposes, such as education, buying a home, or starting a business. The trust also ensures that the wealth is passed down through generations, avoiding premature depletion.

- **Explanation:** This scenario ensures the assets remain protected from external threats such as the children's creditors or potential divorce settlements, preserving the family's wealth for the long term.
- **Trust Term: Preserving Wealth for Future Generations**

Scenario #9

Since David and Regina are expecting another child, any individual who is a direct descendant of the Grantor, whether by birth or legal adoption, shall be automatically considered a beneficiary of this trust. In addition, James is engaged to be married which in turn will facilitate a revision to his family trust.

Any spouse of a direct descendant, upon marriage, may also be included as a beneficiary at the trustee's discretion.

The Trustee shall have the authority to include additional family members as beneficiaries of this Family Trust in connection with the distribution of trust assets. Such individuals may include, but are not limited to, descendants of the Grantor by birth or legal adoption, as well as spouses of direct descendants. The Trustee shall exercise discretion in determining the eligibility of new beneficiaries, taking into consideration the Grantor's intent to provide for the long-term welfare of their family.

- **Explanation:** Any newly added beneficiaries shall be entitled to distributions in accordance with the same terms and conditions applicable to the original beneficiaries unless otherwise specified by the Grantor.
- **Trust Term:** Distributions to Additional Beneficiaries

Summary: These scenarios reflect various goals that a family trust can achieve, from protecting assets for future generations to encouraging education, providing for special needs, supporting a surviving spouse, and preserving wealth. The specific terms will depend on the grantor's objectives, family dynamics, and financial situation.

A family trust helps a family thrive financially by preserving and protecting assets for future generations, ensuring that wealth is managed responsibly and according to the family's long-term goals.

CONCLUSION

The purpose of this journey to next level abundance is to prepare and share a blueprint, template, pattern, or model to illustrate what is possible when you seize available opportunities – with the ultimate opportunity being to create a family legacy.

Creating a "family legacy" refers to the intentional process of building, preserving, and passing down values, traditions, wealth, and accomplishments from one generation to the next. It goes beyond material wealth, encompassing the family's shared vision, moral principles, and contributions to society. A family legacy may include financial stability through carefully managed assets, like trusts or investments, as well as promoting education, philanthropy, and a strong family culture. The concept is about ensuring that future generations benefit not just from monetary resources but also from a lasting impact that reflects the family's identity, purpose, and values.

Made in the USA
Monee, IL
07 November 2026

67974629R00066